Reference

**FACILITY SECURITY PRINCIPLES
FOR NON-SECURITY PRACTIONERS**

Copyright © 2018 Art B. Crow Jr.

Because of the dynamic nature of the Internet, any web addresses or links contained in this book may have changed since publication and may no longer be valid. The views expressed in this work are solely those of the author and do not necessarily reflect the views of the publisher, and the publisher hereby disclaims any responsibility for them.

ISBN-13: 978-1-7321921-0-2

ISBN-10: 1-7321921-0-3

Dedication

This book is dedicated to the thousands of Professional Security Officers the world over who serve as the first line of defense in providing safe and secure workplaces that allow organizations and their employees to achieve great success.

Acknowledgements

Many thanks to Cliff Haller and Craig McQuate for your critique, edits and input. But for your honest feedback and encouragement I would not have been able to complete this book.

Table of Contents

Introduction

In most organizations, including some Fortune 500 companies, direct management oversight of the physical security program is the responsibility of non-security practitioners; facility managers, safety managers and property managers. This is especially true for organizations that do not have a proprietary security department and rely on outsourced security service providers to perform the company's physical security function. This is not to say that non-security practitioners and contract security companies are not capable of providing sound security program management and oversight. Rather, what it does indicate is that the non-security practitioner needs to have a good foundational knowledge of physical security principles and strategies that will allow them to effectively and efficiently lead the corporate security function.

A review of 2 – 4 year college course curricula and professional certification course materials for non-security professionals shows that very little study is dedicated to physical security. Of the course material that is devoted to physical security, the vast majority is limited to an overview of electronic physical security systems; with very little, if any information on physical security concepts and strategies. This leaves the professional facility manager, safety manager or other non-security practitioner no other choice but to learn on the job and rely on their service providers to assess the business' security needs and implement solutions to mitigate any real or perceived risks to the business. Although there are many reputable security service providers and system integrators who provide quality services, there is more to physical security than guards, gates, cameras and door alarms.

Although security needs to provide for the protection of people and property from circumstances and events that could cause serious loss or damage to the organization, it cannot be so restrictive as to impede the business process. Facility security programs need to align with the company's business goals and support business operations at the facility. The security program should also align with the company's corporate culture. Properly aligning the security program with the corporate culture facilitates workforce buy-in, leading to a more effective security posture. When employees and contractors buy into the security culture, they will be more apt to follow and enforce security policy (wear your badge) and report security violations, thefts and suspicious activities, which in turn leads to a more secure and productive workplace. This type of security environment and professional image, especially amongst senior management and decision makers, can also prove to be an invaluable asset when seeking capital improvement and expense funds for systems and program improvements.

It is important to note at the outset that this book is a guide to physical security concepts and principles and is not designed to be a complete reference on all matters related to physical security. The principles, concepts and strategies in this handbook are designed to provide the reader with good foundational knowledge that will assist them in designing and implementing sound physical security programs that align with a company's business model and security needs. Readers wishing to gain more in depth knowledge of physical security are encouraged to consult more focused publications and\or engage the services of a professional security consultant who can assist them in developing a comprehensive facility security program.

Chapter 1

Physical Security Concepts

Purpose of Physical Security

All organizations have a legal *duty of care* to provide a safe and secure workplace for their employees and contractors, as well as provide for the security of company assets and sensitive proprietary and customer information. It can also be reasonably argued that organizations have a duty of care to ensure that their business operations do not pose a significant safety or security risk to the communities in which they operate. If facility security does not act as a deterrent to illicit activities it becomes more likely that an adverse incident will occur on the property. Depending on the severity of the incident, the company may incur financial liability as the result of legal actions or suffer damage to the company's reputation.

Security in its basic form is the protection of property and personnel from circumstances and events that could cause serious loss or damage to an enterprise, agency or institution. That part of security concerned with physical measures is designed to

- Safeguard personnel,
- Prevent unauthorized access to buildings, equipment and information, and
- Safeguard property against espionage, sabotage, damage or theft.

Although the purpose of physical security is quite clear, it is important to note from the outset that absolute protection is impossible to achieve in most environments. Regardless of facility design, security systems deployed and security staffing levels, a determined intruder with the appropriate skills, resources and motivation can gain access to almost any facility. The goal of physical security is to implement reasonable measures to reduce the likelihood of an adverse event occurring.

Physical Security Principles

The principle of physical security is to identify risk exposure – both business and environmental – and develop mitigation strategies to reduce risk exposure. This is accomplished by conducting a facility security assessment to identify real and perceived risks, regulatory\certification requirements, existing protective measures and any gaps in security that may leave the facility vulnerable to external and internal threats. After completing the assessment, the next step is to identify what the company's tolerance is. What is considered to be acceptable and unacceptable risk? From here the manager can begin to identify physical security strategies required to meet the business' needs. More information on facility security assessments is covered in *Chapter 2: Facility Security Assessments.*

After conducting the facility security assessment and identifying acceptable and unacceptable risk, the next step is to develop and implement integrated physical security plans to mitigate that risk and:

- Provide appropriate protection to meet the risk exposure level,
- Combine technology, personnel and guidelines,
- Are not cost prohibitive,
- Are not so restrictive as to impede the business process,
- Are not overly burdensome on the physical security customer, and
- Align with corporate culture.

The key to program success will be how effectively these principles are implemented across the organization and the degree of senior management's buy-in to the program.

Physical Security Responsibilities

Physical security has primary responsibility for protecting facilities and the people and assets within them. This includes the property itself, any structures and the assets within any structure. The 4 principles used to accomplish this are *deter, delay, detect and respond.*

Deter

Deterrence is the concept of designing facilities and properties in such a fashion as to make them undesirable targets for criminal activity. This is most commonly referred to as *Crime Prevention Through Environmental Design (CPTED)*. CPTED takes into consideration the intended use of the facility or space, regulatory requirements, real and perceived risks or threats, and the formulation of design solutions that act as physical and psychological deterrents to intruders. The following are high level strategies that can make a site less desirable for people contemplating illegal activities.[1]

Natural Deterrents define a property's boundaries and\or limit a perpetrator's opportunity for concealment. These include the slope of the property, low edging shrubbery along the property boundary, walkways and building perimeter, and trees. When designing a property's landscape it is important to keep in mind how the landscaping will impact overall security for the property and facility. Clear lines of sight for occupants and legitimate visitors provide them with a better opportunity to observe suspicious persons and behavior and limit opportunity for concealment. Shrubbery and hedging along the building and near entranceways should be placed in such a manner so as not to impede observation of the property from the building interior. Shrubbery along the building perimeter should be no taller than the base of first floor windows and placed no less than 6 feet from the building; reducing the opportunity for concealment between shrubbery and the building. Shrubbery near entranceways should not obstruct a person's ability to view the area outside the doorway. Trees should be placed far enough away from structures to prevent climbing of the tree to gain access to building upper levels and rooftops. Placement should not interfere with CCTV camera views. Trees should be regularly trimmed as they grow to prevent interference with camera views of the property and buildings.

Lighting intensity and area of coverage act as a psychosocial deterrent and enhances the ability to detect unauthorized persons or activities. The appropriate level or intensity of lighting for a site will be dependent on location and risk (i.e., high crime rates, hazardous materials or equipment, etc.). For the most part, standard lighting industry area illumination and light intensity guidelines are sufficient to meet nearly all security lighting requirements. However, there may be certain regulatory requirements on a business that may require a facility to provide higher levels of lighting. Lighting is also an important factor in CCTV camera selection. High-pressure and low-pressure sodium lighting provides poor color rendition for video surveillance and is not recommended for use in security applications. Low light cameras should be used in areas with little to no lighting.

Visible Security in the form of signs, CCTV cameras, security patrols, visible security posts, locks and card reader controlled doors and gates provide an effective deterrent. When planning security tour routes and times, care should be taken not to design predictability into them. Guard tour route and start and end times should be varied as much as possible. Rather than starting the tour at a specific point, have the security officer start at any point along the route. Instead of starting at what is usually the first tour point, the officer could start at the last tour point and work backwards; or start somewhere in the middle. Instead of starting the tour on-the-hour every hour or two, the officer could start the tour at any time 10 – 15 minutes earlier or later than scheduled tour times. The unpredictability of when security will be touring a facility\site helps reduce the likelihood that a predictable pattern can be detected and used by a would-be criminal.

Delay

Delay is accomplished through the use of structural barriers and controls to create physical and psychological deterrents. These include fences, gates, bollards, Jersey barriers, walls, doors, windows, grates, signs and other manufactured devices used to restrict, channel or impede access. Effective delay design layers protective measures that start from the most protected area within a facility and work their way out to the property perimeter. These areas are most commonly identified as *restricted, limited and controlled.*

Restricted areas contain the facility's most critical assets, sensitive information and hazardous processes and materials. These include critical building infrastructure, network infrastructure, data centers, file storage rooms, manufacturing areas, laboratories, high value materials and hazardous materials. These areas require enhanced security measures and should require prior approval before card access or a key is issued to them.

Limited areas are general access areas within a facility that are generally accessible to all authorized employees, contractors, vendors and their visitors. Access to the limited area is controlled through employee badges, staffed access control points, sign-in\out procedures, card readers and mechanical locks.

The *Controlled area* is the property itself and encompasses the grounds and all parking areas and extends to the property line. Access may be controlled by fences, gates or staffed security checkpoints or, it may be an open area where authorized personnel go to and from the facility.

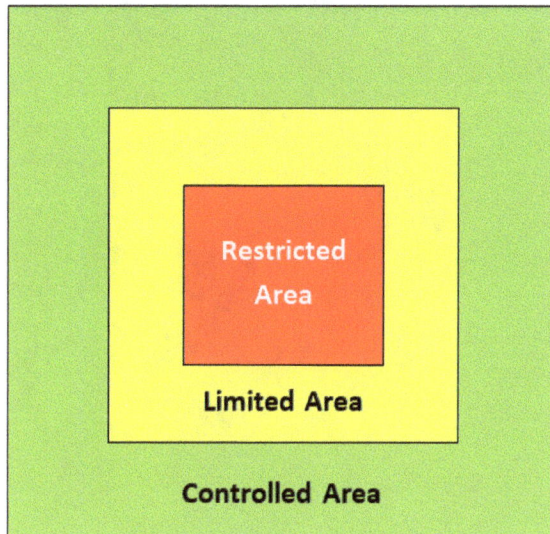

Figure 1: Tiered Security Layer

Detect

Detection is concerned with the electronic physical security systems and security personnel responsible for monitoring the property and facility. All security systems deployed at a facility should be monitored at all times. The access control system should be programmed with door held and forced alarms, as well as access denied alarms that are triggered when card access to an area is rejected because the badge is not programmed for access to the area. CCTV cameras, when properly deployed, allow monitoring personnel to detect suspicious activities and items on the property and within facilities.

Respond

In order for security to be effective there must be a mechanism in place for response to security alarms, suspicious activities, criminal acts and emergency conditions. Information on security procedures is discussed in more detail in *Chapter 2, The Facility Security Assessment* and *Chapter 3, Policies, Standards and Procedures.*

Chapter 2

Facility Security Plans

The facility security plan is a comprehensive document that identifies the risks inherent to an organization and its facility(s) and the strategies and resources (systems, personnel, equipment, and procedural controls) required to mitigate those risks. Plan development should be a cross functional effort with input from multiple business unit mangers and address specific identifiable risks with cost-effective solutions that support business goals and reduce risk exposure.

An effective means to develop a security plan involves a 4 phased approach:

Phase 1:   Identification of critical assets.

Phase 2:   Conducting a facility security assessment to identify business and environmental risks.

Phase 3:   Developing risk management strategies to address risk exposure.

Phase 4:   Developing a security budget that aligns with business and security plan objectives.

Critical Asset Identification

Identification of critical assets is a key element of security plan development as it sets the baseline from which levels of protection for the facility will be formulated. Critical assets are any assets that if lost, damaged or compromised could have a significant negative impact on the business. These include physical and logical assets and information that is critical to the business processes and allow a company to remain competitive in their market and maintain a safe and secure work environment. They include but are not limited to:

- Product designs and proprietary formulas

- Manufacturing and processing schematics and equipment

- Prototype equipment and materials

- Critical building and network infrastructure

- Hazardous materials

- Sensitive personnel information

Loss of product designs, formulas and manufacturing and processing information to a competitor can significantly impact the ability of the company to maintain a market advantage. Damage to critical building infrastructure or network information systems can shut down facility and business operations until repairs are made and the systems are brought back on line. Release of hazardous materials has the potential to have a negative impact on the facility, the local community and environment, as well as the company's reputation.

Facility Security Assessment

The facility security assessment identifies the core business and operating model at a facility or site, the regulatory requirements on the business, any risks inherent to the business itself and any outside influences that may have an impact on or pose a risk or threat to the business and its personnel and assets. These include environmental risks such as local area crime rates, frequency and severity of natural disasters or extreme weather events and proximity to potentially hazardous sites (chemical processing and storage facilities, facility is in airport flight path, adjacent to railroad line, etc.). The assessment also looks at existing facility protection measures and makes recommendations, where necessary, to improve levels of protection to reduce risk exposure. More detailed information on facility security assessments is contained in *Chapter 3, Facility Security Assessments.*

Risk Management Strategies

After information on critical assets and processes has been gathered and a facility security assessment has been completed, the next step is to develop strategies to manage identified risks. Organizations may choose one or more approaches to risk management. The four common approaches are:

Risk Acceptance: Risk acceptance does not reduce any risk exposure and is a common option when the cost of other risk management options may outweigh the impact of the risk itself. This approach is commonly used when a risk event does not have a high possibility of occurring or if the impact of an event would have a negligible adverse impact on the company. If risk acceptance is the approach to an identified risk, the risk and reason(s) for acceptance should be documented.

Risk Avoidance: Risk avoidance is an action that avoids any exposure to the risk. Risk avoidance is usually the most expensive of all risk mitigation options as it usually entails changing a business model or relocating a facility in order to avoid risk exposure.

Risk Reduction: Risk reduction seeks to limit a company's exposure by allocating resources to reduce risk exposure and\or limit the adverse impact an event may have on the company. An example of risk reduction would be limiting access to sensitive proprietary information, hazardous materials or critical infrastructure.

Risk Transference: Risk transference involves passing risk off to a third party. An example of this would be a pharmaceutical company that has R&D laboratories, but outsources animal testing to a contract research organization (CRO). The risk of animal rights extremists showing up at the facility is less likely than if the company does not perform tests on laboratory animals at the facility. This is also a viable option that can allow a company to focus more on their core competencies while still meeting overall business objectives.

Risk management strategies predominantly employ a cost-benefit analysis approach to identify the cost of a particular strategy to reduce risk or vulnerability to specific assets and processes. The cost of the recommended strategy is weighed against the risk, its likelihood of occurrence and the potential impact on the organization should the event occur. An effective means to measure risk probability and potential impact is the use of a risk assessment matrix (Figure 2). The likelihood of an adverse event is rated from very unlikely to very likely and the impact is listed from negligible to extreme; with ratings of low, medium, high and critical assigned each risk category\type. The advantage of using the risk assessment matrix is that risks that may have otherwise been considered as low due to a low likelihood of occurrence may actually prove to be a high risk due to the potential adverse impact should the event occur. An example of this would be a network breach. Although a company may have a good firewall, antivirus and antimalware software and sound IT user protocols, making it unlikely that a breach would occur, if a hacker was able to hack into company information systems and compromise sensitive company or client information, the impact could be high or critical, making this a high or critical risk.

	IMPACT				
PROBABILITY	NEGLIGIBLE	MINOR	MODERATE	MAJOR	EXTREME
VERY LIKELY	MEDIUM 2	HIGH 3	HIGH 3	CRITICAL 4	CRITICAL 4
LIKELY	MEDIUM 2	MEDIUM 2	HIGH 3	HIGH 3	CRITICAL 4
POSSIBLE	LOW 1	MEDIUM 2	MEDIUM 2	HIGH 3	CRITICAL 4
UNLIKELY	LOW 1	MEDIUM 2	MEDIUM 2	MEDIUM 2	HIGH 3
VERY UNLIKELY	LOW 1	LOW 1	MEDIUM 2	MEDIUM 2	HIGH 3

Figure 2: Risk Assessment Matrix

While each business may have specific risks associated with their business model, there are common risks that many businesses face based on their geographical location and environment. The table at Figure 3 lists some of the most common risks posted to businesses. It is recommended that other categories be added to this list and include risks inherent to the business itself. i.e., companies with large amounts of hazardous materials have an increased risk of chemical release; companies with hazardous operations or machinery have an increased risk of personal injury.

Risk\Threat	Probability	Impact	Risk Score	Notes
Area Crime Rate				Number and frequency of crimes against the person and property crimes and number of level 3 sex offenders within 1 mile of the facility.
Property Damage				Number and frequency of property damage and vandalism incidents.
Civil Unrest				Riots and protests against major socio-political issues.
Strike\Demonstration				Organized labor protests and demonstrations against company because of its business model or associations.
Outsider Theft				Number of break and enter and property theft incidents including, vehicle theft, theft from vehicles by non-site personnel. Area crime rates and internal company incidents reports should be reviewed.
Insider Theft				Company and personal property theft by employees and onsite contractors.
Information\Data Theft				Theft of logical and physical information.
Extreme Weather Events				Tornadoes, hurricanes, blizzards, hail storms, etc.
Natural Disasters				Earthquakes, flooding, wildfires, etc.
Workplace Violence				Incidents of threats or physical altercations in the workplace.
Terrorism				Domestic and international terrorism.

Figure 3: General Risk Categories

Using the risk assessment matrix, each risk should be given at rating of low, medium, high or critical. Risks rated as critical and high should always be addressed first. Risks rated as low and medium should be addressed after all high and critical risks have been addressed. After risks have been rated, the next step is to develop strategies to mitigate them and identify the cost-benefit of each strategy.

An effective cost-benefit analysis should include a cost to recover from an adverse event if it were to occur. If a critical piece of equipment is damaged or stolen, how much would it cost the company to recover from the loss? If a significant event occurs that results in the shutdown of business operations at the facility, what would be the cost in lost revenue due to the shutdown? This information is essential in justifying security capital and expense budgets.

Businesses normally assign a dollar value (*Loss Value*) to all losses or potential losses. Regardless of what the loss may be (theft, property damage, etc.), there will always be a value assigned to it. Whenever a business experiences a loss it must generate additional revenue to recover from that loss (*Cost to Recover*). A method for determining cost to recover for critical assets and processes is to assign a loss value to the asset\process and then determine what additional revenue would be required to the replace the asset and\or recover from an event. A simple formula to determine cost to recover is to divide the loss value by the company's after-tax net profit percentage (*ATNP%*).

$$\frac{Loss\ Value}{ATNP\ \%} = Cost\ to\ Recover$$

Using this formula we can show a return on investment dollar value in terms of additional revenue required to recover from a loss event. If a company with a 4.35% ATNP experiences the loss of a piece of equipment valued at $25,000, the company would need generate to $574,713 in additional revenue to recover from the loss.

$$\frac{\$25,000}{4.35\ \%} = \$574,713$$

If the argument is that the company has an insurance policy that covers losses due to theft, property damage and business interruption, applying the same formula to the insurance policy deductible can show additional revenue that would be required to recover from the deductible before the insurance company would payout on the claim. Let's assume the company has a $5,000,000 policy that includes a theft and property damage rider. Since business insurance providers normally require a minimum 1% - 2% deductible on all business policies, we'll assume the company's deductible rate is 1.5%.

$$Deductiblte = \$5,000,000 \times 1.5\% = \$75,000$$

$$\frac{\$75,000}{4.35\,\%} = \$1,724,138$$

This shows that even though a company may have an insurance policy, the actual cost to recover from a loss event is significantly more than the cost of the policy deductible.

Quantifying cost to recover in this manner can greatly assist managers in prioritizing levels of protection for a facility. After workplace safety, resource allocation should be prioritized based on cost to recover dollar value. Risks with the highest cost to recover value should receive the highest priority for resource allocation; with lower risks receiving lesser priority. This approach can prove to be an invaluable tool when developing reasonable and sustainable security budgets that are in alignment with business objectives.

An example of an effective strategy to reduce the risk of insider theft of high value scrap materials from a manufacturing process might be to have all high value scrap materials stored in a caged area within the facility, use a card reader to control access to the cage and install a CCTV camera to monitor the area. The cost-benefit analysis in this instance would be to compare the value of the scrap material to the cost of the systems being installed. Using the cost to recover formula previously discussed, we can determine whether or not the installation of the storage cage, card reader and CCTV camera are beneficial or not.

Assuming a manufacturing plant has scrap materials that average $2,000,000 annually and the average shrinkage rate for their industry is 1%, the potential annual loss value is $20,000 ($2,000,000 x .01). Using the same ATNP of 4.35%, the additional revenue required to recover from the loss would be $459,770. If it cost $15,000 to install the cage, card reader and CCTV camera, the installation far outweighs the potential annual loss; $15,000 invested to save a potential $459,770 in recurring annual revenue loss.

While it is relatively easy to measure the tangible impacts that security can have on the bottom line, other impacts that are as equally important are sometimes more difficult to quantify. These may include:

- Reduced productivity

- Potential lost sales and income

- Compliance and regulatory audits

- Customer satisfaction and retention

- Business partner dissatisfaction or retention

- Delay of new business plans

Taking a team approach and working with other business unit managers across the organization will help the security program manager identify potential risks and develop reasonable risk management strategies to reduce the negative impacts on the company should an adverse event occur.

Budget Development

The security budget should include all risk management strategies outlined in the facility security plan and the costs associated with all resources required to implement those strategies. These include but are not limited to:

- Electronic physical security systems (access control, intrusion detection, CCTVs, visitor management system, etc.)

- Security staffing (contract and\or proprietary)

- Space utilization requirements

- Computers and IT resources

- Security equipment and vehicles, including maintenance and fuel costs

- Locks and keys

- Door hardware

- Lighting

- Gates, gate arms and fencing

- Employee and contractor training

Consideration also needs to be given to maintenance and annual licensing fees associated with security systems and equipment. As is the case with other building management systems, physical security systems require regularly scheduled maintenance to ensure they remain operationally functional as designed and installed. For product life-cycle planning purposes, the average life-cycle for all electronic physical security system hardware components (locks, card readers, door contacts, CCTV cameras, etc.) is 7 years.

It is important to note that the final decision on whether or not the plan is adequate and what strategies and resources may or may not be acceptable to mitigate risk lays with the senior decision makers within the organization; not the security program manager. After the facility security plan and budget have been developed they will need to be submitted to company senior management, risk management and\or procurement for review and approval.

The information contained in the following chapters provide more detail on facility physical security concepts that can be used for developing baseline levels of protect and facility security plans. Appendix A, Facility Protection Measures provides baseline system recommendations for securing company facilities.

Chapter 3

Facility Security Assessments

The purpose of the physical security assessment is to identify the core business and operating model at a facility or site, the regulatory requirements on the business, any risks inherent to the business itself and any outside influences that may have an adverse impact on or pose a risk to the business and its personnel and assets. Understanding these factors provides security program managers with the knowledge required to develop and implement security strategies and methodologies that align with the business's overall objectives, initiatives and culture. From a legal perspective, the assessment also serves as a *logical audit trail* and proof of what the company has done to identify and mitigate risk; which could prove useful in any legal action, insurance claim or regulatory audit.

A physical security assessment should be conducted whenever:

- A new facility or site is planned,

- Requesting capital or expense funds for program improvements,

- Significant changes are made to the business' operating model at a facility or site,

- Certification through a regulatory body or agency is planned,

- Using a third party vendor to manufacture, transport and\or store company materials or finished products, or

- Significant enhancement or changes to the physical security program are required as the result of a major event that has had a negative impact on business operations or the facility.

Assessments should not be a one-and-done type of thing. Many organizations, including government agencies, have a tendency to fall into the mindset that if nothing has gone wrong for a long period of time, reassessment of risks and program audit are not really necessary. Quite to the contrary, the constantly changing aspects of the business environment and advancements in security technology require continual assessment of risk and program fundamentals to ensure the physical security program is providing optimal protection to the facility. While initial assessments should be detailed and encompass all aspects of the business, facilities, assets and risks, follow up assessments can be tailored to focus on key aspects of the security program, with recommendations for technology and process improvement. As a general guideline, follow up physical security assessments should be conducted every 3 – 5 years or upon major facility or security system redesign or upgrade. Assessments of 3rd party vendor facilities and security operations should be conducted every 1 – 2 years; depending on the criticality of the research, manufacturing, transportation or storage services they are providing.

Assessments should be conducted by an experienced security consultant or an experienced security professional; whether in-house or contracted. Oftentimes, it is better to use a security consultant who can provide an "outsider's" perspective of the program, as using your security service provider can present a possible conflict of interest and unintended bias. A written assessment report outlining all identified risks, observations made, program strengths and improvement recommendations should always be completed by the assessor and provided to the company at the conclusion of the assessment.

Following are suggested site information and minimum security program areas that should be reviewed as part of a comprehensive physical security assessment. An organization's business model will dictate whether the assessment should be broadened to encompass more operational aspects of the facility.

Business & Site Information

General information on the site(s) being assessed provides the assessment team with the basic information upon which the assessment is built. This information includes, but is not limited to:

- Business name (including D.B.A, if applicable)
- Physical Address
- Type of business

- Primary business functions of the site (manufacturing, office, R&D laboratories, warehousing, etc.)

- Number of years in business

- Number of employees

- Normal business hours

- Shift schedules

- Site map\plan

- Floorplans

Regulatory\Certification Requirements

Regulatory requirements and any certifications the business holds can have a significant impact on a business' security program. Regulatory requirements can be defined as any federal, state or local laws or regulations that mandate minimum safety and\or security standards applicable to business or its facilities. Similarly, certification requirements refer to any regulatory body or agency physical security requirements a business must meet to obtain and\or maintain any industry or program certification. Not meeting regulatory or certification security requirements can have a significant negative impact on the business; ranging from an inability to obtain certification to loss of certification, damage to company reputation and, in the most severe cases, loss of customers, shutdown of business operations at the site, fines and possible civil law suits and criminal prosecution.

It is incumbent upon managers of company physical security programs to understand the regulatory, certification and audit requirements of the organization and what role physical security plays in them. It is also important to note that the audit\inspection process begins the moment the auditor or inspector steps on the property. The first impression set by security at the main entrance will undoubtedly set the tone for the rest of the audit.

Although not all inclusive, following are some examples of common regulatory and certification requirements with physical security implications.

National Fire Protection Association Life Safety Code (NFPA-101)[2], *International Building Code IBC 1008.1.4.4*[3] and local building codes provide specific guidelines on access controlled egress doors, including electrified door hardware, electromagnetic locks, sensors, emergency door release buttons, door unlock timing and integration of access controlled doors with the building's fire protection system. These standards are normally incorporated in local building fire and life safety codes.

29 CFR 1910, U.S. Occupational Health & Safety Administration (OSHA), Uniform Building Code and NFPA provide strict guidelines on the handling, storage and disposal of hazardous materials. Physical security controls on the delivery and storage of hazardous materials should be included in security standards and procedures.[4]

29 CFR 1910.38, U.S. Occupational Health & Safety Administration (OSHA) requires employers to develop emergency action plans to "address emergencies that the employer may reasonably expect in the workplace."[5] Security is an integral part of the business' emergency response team and security's emergency response procedures need to align with facility and business unit emergency response protocols.

21 CFR outlines federally mandated Food and Drug Administration (FDA) regulations on the manufacture, storage and distribution of food, drugs and medical device products. Although the strictest physical security guidelines can be found in the CFR 21, Chapter II relating to the manufacture, storage and distribution of controlled substances, other chapters outline minimum security requirements and how access to information and product is controlled. Even minor security non-compliance with FDA regulations can have a negative impact on the organization, including fines and suspension of business operations until the variance is resolved satisfactorily.[6]

Customs Trade Partnership Against Terrorism (CTPAT) is a voluntary program between U.S. Customs and Border Patrol (CBP) and private industry to strengthen international supply chain security. A significant portion of the certification and audit process focuses on access control, key control and electronic physical security systems. Organizations that participate in the CTPAT program experience less cargo inspection wait times at U.S. ports of entry; thereby reducing warehousing costs and material and product delivery times. CBP conducts random audits to validate compliance with CTPAT guidelines.[7]

Statement on Standards for Attestation Engagements (SSAE) No. 18 is primarily applicable to the financial industry and "requires companies to take more control and ownership of their own internal controls around the identification and classification of risk and appropriate management of third party vendor relationships." To this extent, "service organizations will need to implement a formal third party vendor management program' and ...'will need to implement a formal annual risk assessment process." System and Organization Controls (SOC) 2 evaluates the organization's information controls relevant to security, availability, processing integrity, confidentiality and\or privacy. Part of the information security controls evaluated includes how physical access to the areas housing information systems is controlled and monitored. This includes how access is requested, approved and removed, physical access control system applications, card readers and dual authentication, alarm monitoring and response, CCTV cameras, systems maintenance, business resiliency of the systems and key control. Additionally, third party vendor or "sub-service organization" – systems integrator and security services provider – practices are also auditable. It has become common practice in the financial and insurance industries for prospective corporate customers to conduct a due diligence SSAE-18 audit prior to signing a service agreement, and existing customers to conduct random audits during the contract's service period.[8]

International Organization for Standardization (ISO) 27001 and 27002 on information security standards provides specific guidance on physical and environmental security controls for areas housing business information systems. In order for a business to maintain ISO 27001/27002 certification they must consistently maintain these standards, which must be internally audited on an annual basis. The business is also subject to random ISO surveillance and re-certification audits.[9]

Transportation Asset Protection Association (TAPA) Certification. TAPA is "a worldwide coalition of manufacturers, shippers, carriers, insurers, service providers, law enforcement and government agencies,' and 'includes every type of company or organization facing the problem of cargo crime within the transportation supply chain." TAPA has developed supply chain security standards and provides a rigorous certification process for the transportation and storage of manufactured goods.[10]

Natural Environment

Although you may have little to no control over the environment the business is located in, it is important to note the risks inherent to that environment that could have an adverse impact on business operations. Is the facility\site located in an area susceptible to serve weather conditions? Hurricanes, tornados, flooding, high winds, lightening, blizzards? What are the instances of earthquakes and forest fires? There are also manmade features and disasters that need to be taken into consideration. What is the site's proximity to facilities that manufacture or store large quantities of flammable or hazardous materials? Is the site located near railroad tracks or in an airport's flight path? What is the proximity to emergency services such as fire department, police department and hospitals?

Crime & Incident Rates

High levels of theft, property damage, vandalism and crimes against the person in the site's immediate vicinity will inherently increase the risk level to the business and its personnel and assets. High larceny\theft rates indicate a higher risk of property theft. High assault and robbery rates indicate a higher risk of crimes against the person. A history of arson and bomb threats could be an indicator of potential domestic\international terrorist activities. Additionally, a systemic issue with internal incidents of property theft, property damage, threats or workplace violence could indicate vulnerabilities in the physical security program that may need to be addressed to reduce the likelihood of incident recurrence.

Labor Disputes, Civil Unrest & Activist Activities

Does the business have a unionized workforce? If yes, what has the history of management's relationship with the union been? Have there been any strikes, walkouts or lockouts within the past 5 years? What impact did any labor disputes have on the business?

Similarly, is the business' industry sector at the center of or target of any activist or extremist group activities? Have any activist groups ever sent any threatening communications to the company or any of its employees? Have any groups showed up at the company or at an employee's residence? If yes, did they attempt to gain access or cause any property damage? Are any of the company's suppliers or service providers the target of any group? Known as tertiary targeting, this is a tactic widely used by many animal rights activist groups where they target a company's business partners in an effort to get them to stop doing business with a company that uses their products or services. An example of this is the Animal Liberation Front (ALF) targeting FedEx and UPS because they provided services to pharmaceutical companies that performed tests on laboratory animals.

Incidents of civil unrest also pose a risk to the business. If the business in located in an area with a frequent history of protests or riots, the risk of property damage, theft and personal injury will be significantly higher than if the facility was located outside one of these areas.

Physical Security

This portion of the assessment focuses on the physical security measures implemented by the business to deter, delay, detect and respond to unauthorized or criminal activity noted in *Chapter 1, The Concept of Physical Security*: natural deterrents, structural deterrents, lighting and visible security controls. Do the measures implemented at the site act as an effective deterrent and are effective response measures in place, or do they need improvement?

Electronic Security Systems and Monitoring

Are the electronic physical security systems at the site sufficient to provide protection to the business? Is the system up-to-date with modern technology? Are the access control and CCTV systems integrated? Does the business have a software support agreement (SSA) with the system(s) manufacturer? Are regular patches installed\applied to the applications and system servers? Is regular testing and maintenance performed on the systems? Does the business have an installation, maintenance and service agreement with a security system integrator certified to install and maintain the systems? Are security systems monitored?

Security Force Staffing & Training

Who within the organization has overall responsibility for physical security program management and oversight? What is the makeup of the security force? 100% proprietary staff; a mixture of proprietary and contract personnel; 100% contract security? What is the pre-employment screening process for security personnel? Is the staffing level sufficient to meet business operational needs? Does it allow for effective access control, building patrols, systems monitoring and incident response? Does the supervisor to security officer ratio allow for effective staff supervision? Are security officers required to be certified in First Aid\ AED\CPR? Do security personnel receive training in general security responsibilities and site\position specific duties and responsibilities? Is the training documented? Are regular emergency procedures drills conducted to ensure security personnel maintain proficiency in emergency response procedures?

Procedural Guidelines

Procedural guidelines outline the strategies and methods used by the business to secure its property, personnel and assets. They include accepted policies, standards and procedures that form the foundation of the physical security program. Do the policies, procedures and standards in place align with business initiatives and operations? Do the protocols align with any regulatory, statutory and certification requirements on the business? Are there procedures in place for response to routine and emergency incidents? Are the procedures at security posts proprietary or contractor provided procedures? Is there a key management system in place? More information on procedural controls can be found in *Chapter 4: Policies, Standards and Procedures*.

Chapter 4

Policies, Standards and Procedures

As previously stated, security policies, standards and procedures are the guidelines that outline the strategies and methods used by a business to secure its property, personnel and assets. Policies provide broad guidance on security program principles and are accepted by senior management; standards provide specific guidance on how physical security strategies and methods are to be implemented across the organization; procedures provide guidelines on day-to-day security operations and activities. The guidelines you implement should align with business needs and incorporate any regulatory, statutory or certification requirements on the business, as well as any customer dictated minimum security requirements.

In all instances, whether policy, standards or procedures, the goal is to achieve consistency across the organization. Reasonable risk based security protocols that are applied uniformly across the organization and are applicable to all sites and personnel, including senior management, provide a consistent security experience at whichever company facility people may visit and reinforce the corporate security culture. The security consumer (employees, contractors and visitors) will be more likely to comply with security protocols if the security is consistent across the organization.

Policies

Corporate security policies should set the overall purpose and objectives of the physical security program and explain in general terms what is expected of security and the security consumer. As a general rule, policy documents should be limited to 1 page, with the meat of the policy outlined in 1 - 3 paragraphs. Obviously, organizations subject to regulatory controls may require more than 1 page to outline corporate policy. However, the basic policy rule should still apply;

it should provide broad guidelines and not include the day-to-day operational aspects of the security program. Following are examples of language that can be used to convey corporate physical security policy.

Access Control Policy

[Company Name] operates its facilities as secure facilities; meaning that unrestricted access to company property and facilities is not authorized. This includes all company owned or leased property or spaces. To this extent:

- [Company Name] Security shall implement electronic, mechanical, and procedural controls to facilitate business access needs and that restrict access to company facilities and assets to authorized personnel only.

- Everyone entering a company facility must present a valid [Company Name] issued photo identification (ID) badge or be signed in and escorted at all times by a valid badge holder. ID badges must be worn on the person's outer most garment at all times while within company facilities.

- Access to restricted areas shall be limited to only those persons with a verifiable business need for access. Unescorted or badge access to any restricted area must be approved by the designated person(s) responsible for approving access to that area.

Key Control Policy

[Company Name] Security shall be the sole authority for the implementation and administration of the company Key Control Program. In the case of remote offices or locations, Security may delegate site key control program administration to a management level employee responsible for site or business unit management.

- Keys shall only be issued on a business need basis and then, only when other means of access, such as card readers, alphanumeric PIN pads or biometric readers are not available.

- The distribution of master keys shall be kept to an absolute minimum and be limited to Facilities, Safety and Security personnel who require access to multiple areas within a facility during the normal course of their day-to-day job related duties.

- Master keys shall not be removed from company property without written authorization of [Company Name] Security or the person responsible site key control program administration.

- Keys are not to be loaned by the authorized key holder to another person to facilitate that person's access to a key controlled area.

- The duplication of company keys by anyone other than the key control program administrator is prohibited.

Company keys remain the property of the company and must be surrendered whenever the purpose for which they were issue is no longer valid, a person terminates their employment or no longer works at the site, or whenever requested to do so by Security or the key control program administrator.

Internal Investigations Policy

[Company Name] reserves the right to investigate improprieties in the workplace that violate any company policies or procedures, regulatory guidelines, applicable law, or pose a risk to a safe and secure workplace.

[Company Name] Security, Legal and Human Resources shall implement guidelines for conducting internal company investigations and function as a team in all internal investigative efforts. Internal investigations that indicate a need to notify law enforcement shall first be reviewed and approved by the corporate legal team before such notification is made.

All employees, contractors, vendors and visitors are expected to cooperate with company investigative efforts. Any person who refuses to cooperate with any company investigation, whether internal or external, shall be subject disciplinary action; up to and including termination of employment or termination of contract. Visitors who do not cooperate with investigative efforts may be banned from returning to company property.

As you can see, the preceding sample policy statements provide a broad, but clear overview of company expectations from which more detailed standards and procedures can be developed.

Facility Security Standards

Facility security standards provide guidelines or specifications on how physical security measures are to be implemented across an organization. They differ from security procedures in that they address the strategy, systems and methodology for implementing physical security controls; whereas security procedures are more focused on day-to-day security activities. Facility security standards should reference and incorporate company security policy and any regulatory, statutory or certification requirements inherent to the business.

When developing standards, it is best to refer back to the physical security concepts discussed in Chapter 1. The standards you develop should outline the controls the company is implementing to deter, delay, detect and respond to unauthorized or criminal activity.

Property and Facility Structures

The best approach for developing standards for properties and structures is to think of them in terms of a construction specifications document. What is the purpose of the standard or control, what are the specifications on the materials to be used and how are they to be installed and maintained? The following are general security standard considerations:

- Detailed landscaping requirements. How should the physical landscape be contoured? Shrubbery and trees positioned throughout the property should not impede clear lines of sight and CCTV camera views. Trimming should be performed at regular intervals to maintain clear lines of sight.

- If the property will have a perimeter fence, provide specifications on the type of fence and where and how it is to be installed. Chain-link fences should be constructed with 9-gauge or heavier galvanized wire with mesh openings no larger than 2 inches and have galvanized rails or twisted selvages at the top and the bottom. Fences should be 8′ in height and securely fastened to rigid metal or reinforced-concrete posts set in concrete, which should be no more than 10′ – 12′ on center.

- If there are parking structures or lots, how will access to them be controlled? If using mechanical or electrified gates or gate arms, provide gate specifications, including make, model and installation guidelines.

- Exterior loading dock areas should be segregated from other areas of the property and vehicular access to them should be controlled.

- List specifications for exterior and interior security lighting.

- If windows will be tinted, include tinting specifications. Tinting should not impede the ability of people inside the building from viewing exterior areas.

Doors and Door Hardware

This section identifies the minimum standard door, hardware and locking specifications for perimeter and restricted area doors. Doors and door hardware should meet the same UL fire rating specification as doors normally used during construction and retrofit projects; hollow metal doors, solid core wood doors, glass doors, storefront configurations, etc. In some instances, such as facilities that manufacture drugs or perform government or military R&D or manufacturing, doors may also have to meet minimum tooled entry resistance specifications that inhibit tampering and\or minimum time specifications on resistance to the use of tools to breach the door. Examples of these include:

- Perimeter doors – Hollow metal, glass and storefront configurations.

- Interior data centers and IDF\MDF rooms – Hollow metal or solid wood core.

- File storage rooms – Solid wood core.

- Building infrastructure (electrical, mechanical, fire suppression, etc.) – Hollow metal.

- Laboratories – Hollow metal or solid wood core.

- Perimeter, stairwell and restricted area doors should be fitted with door closers.

- Single doors with standard locksets or electric strikes should be fitted with latch guards.

- Double doors should be fitted with door astragals.

- Perimeter doors should be fitted with security hinges that hinder the ability to remove the door if hinge pins are removed or the hinge is cut.

Electronic Physical Security Systems

Outline the acceptable security system applications, component parts, where and how they are to be installed and how systems are to be monitored. Include information on the electronic security measures to be used for securing the building perimeter and functional business areas – data centers, IDF\MDF rooms, building infrastructure areas, laboratories, file storage rooms, etc. Following are general guidelines on information that should be included in this section. More detailed information on electronic physical security systems and systems design is discussed in *Chapter 5, Electronic Physical Security Systems.*

- The same access control and CCTV platforms should be used at all company facilities. Divergent systems across the business inhibit the ability to integrate them. It also requires company security personnel to monitor multiple security applications or, in the case of outsourced security systems monitoring, may require multiple vendors to monitor the different applications; which in turn increases security's cost of doing business.

- The vetting process for security system integrators.

  - What systems should they be certified in and how much experience should they have?

  - If there are disparate systems, does the integrator have experience integrating these systems to achieve optimal performance?

- The company's preferred access control system platform.

- The devices – carder readers, biometric readers, PIN pads, alarm contacts, glass break sensors, door release buttons, electrified transfer hinges, etc. - by make and model number that are to be used and how they should be installed (i.e., in accordance with International Building Code IBC 1008.1.4.4., American with Disabilities Act, etc.).

- Recommended door unlock timing for valid cards reads, request to exit device activation, door release buttons and systems operator momentary door unlocks.

- Integration with the building's fire protection system.

- The company's preferred video management (CCTV) system.

- Acceptable CCTV cameras, by make and model numbers and where and how should they be installed.

  - Care should be taken in determining camera area coverage so as not to violate any legal or collective bargaining agreement on workplace monitoring guidelines.

  - Businesses should not use cameras with audio recording capabilities without first checking applicable federal, state and local wiretap laws.

- It is recommended that businesses not use "dummy" CCTV cameras. Dummy cameras serve no other purpose than a visual deterrent which could lead to a false sense of security and legal liability issues.

- Minimum recorded video retention time. 30 days, 60 days, 90 days, 180 days? While 30 – 60 day retention is acceptable in many environments, regulated environments may mandate longer video retention times.

- How the access control and video management systems are to be integrated.

- Standard naming conventions for doors, security devices and CCTV cameras.

  - Standard naming conventions make it easier for systems monitoring personnel to identify the location of doors and devices in alarm; as well as which cameras to bring up when an event occurs. A good format is to use building numbers, floor\door number, door\area name, and alarm\device type. i.e., 35-1436-Hazmat Storage Room-Held, indicates that the door in alarm is the hazmat storage room located on the 1st floor of building 35, the room number is 1436 and the door is being held open; 45-1228-Glass Break Sensor, indicates the glass break sensor in room 1228 on the 1st floor of building 45 has been activated. Naming cameras in the same manner and associating the camera name with the area being monitoring with allow security to bring up the appropriate camera more quickly for alarm response or investigative purposes.

- Systems' primary and backup power supply requirements.

  - Physical security systems should always be connected to the building UPS and\or emergency generator circuit. Security panels and device power supplies hour also have a minimum 4-hour internal battery backup power supply.

- Recommended preventative maintenance checks and services (PMCS) schedule for access control system devices and CCTV cameras.

  - What is to be checked, how should it be checked and how often should it be checked?

  - At what point should devices or CCTV cameras be replaced?

- As a minimum, door alarms and access control system devices should be checked at least quarterly by onsite security or facilities personnel to ensure system functionality. CCTV cameras should be checked daily to ensure they are functioning properly.

- The preferred security systems integrator should complete annual systems checks, clean and adjust component parts, and replace defective parts on an as needed basis.

- How and when application software patches should be applied.

  - Businesses should obtain and keep current a software support agreement (SSA) for the security system applications they use. SSA's allow system owners to receive application updates to maintain system functionality.

  - It is not uncommon for IT to require patches to be run in a test environment prior to installation on production servers. General information on IT systems patching guidelines should be included in this section.

- Who, by position title, will have administrative and\or monitoring rights for the access control and video management systems?

- How will systems be monitored and by whom?

Lock and Key Systems

Outline in detail the types of locks and the key system to be used on all doors. Examples are:

- Locksets, mortise locksets, storage room and passage sets.

- Keyways and keys

  - Keyways should be interchangeable cores. This makes it easier and less expensive over the long when changing locks as a result of keys that have been lost, stolen or not returned.

  - Only company padlocks or cable locks should be used to secure company areas or equipment; such as fence gates and grounds keeping equipment.

  - All locks and keyways should be pinned in accordance with the company key hierarchy. Note: The key hierarchy should not be included in the facility security standards document. It is a sensitive security document that should be treated as confidential proprietary information.

- Locks, interchangeable cores and keys should only be ordered and\or pinned\cut by the company's authorized locksmith.

- Each site should have someone designated as a primary and alternate key control authority or administrator with authority for implementing and administering the site's key control program.

More information on key hierarchy design and mechanical locking systems is discussed in *Chapter 5, Key Management Program.*

Access Control

How will access to the property, parking structures, buildings and restricted areas be controlled? This should include guidelines on minimum staffing requirements for personnel and loading dock entrances.

- All building perimeter and personnel entrance doors should be staffed with a security officer or receptionist whenever the door is unlocked or open for an extended period of time (i.e., construction, equipment moves, etc.).

- Personnel without a valid company issued ID badge should be signed in and escorted at all times while in company facilities.

- For manufacturing and distribution center facilities, there should be a segregated waiting area for truck drivers to wait while their trucks are being loading or unloaded. It should have:

  - A connected shipping and receiving office with a clerk's window for processing shipments with drivers,

  - A door leading into the warehouse that is locked from the waiting room area side,

  - Chairs and small tables for reading materials,

  - A bathroom, and

  - A Television (budget permitting)

- Restrictions on loading dock area parking.

- Parking garage and lot access controls.

- Access to areas containing hazardous materials, equipment\machinery or processes.

- Access to high value materials, including scrap and production waste.

- The types of locks to be used on restricted area security doors, areas or equipment.

  - Mortise locksets on perimeter doors.

  - Mortise or standard locksets for interior stairwells, infrastructure and restricted area doors.

  - Standard locksets for offices and storage rooms.

  - Electrified and electromagnetic locks.

  - Card readers, biometric readers and\or PIN pads for restricted area doors.

    - Some regulations and standards require two factor authentication to gain access to data centers, telecomm rooms and other restricted areas within a facility.

Security Staffing and Training

This section is primarily concerned with contract security service providers, vetting providers, security staff pre-employment\assignment screening and officer training requirements. If the business has a master services agreement (MSA) with a preferred security services provider, the MSA should dictate requirements that apply across the organization. If the provider is using a subcontractor to provide services in an area where they do not have a physical presence, the MSA should outline the subcontractor's requirement to meet the same service requirements outlined in the MSA signed by the preferred service provider, and a stipulation that the primary contractor is responsible for the subcontractor's performance standards. Wherever possible, the following guidelines should also be included in the security services MSA.

- Pre-employment screening should include, as a minimum:

  - Verification of authorization to work in the U.S. or applicable country.

- Verification of social security (social insurance) number through E-Verify or applicable verification process.

- 5 years employment history verification. More may be required based on regulatory or state requirements inherent to the business.

- Pre-employment drug screening for drugs of abuse; where applicable law permits.

- Minimum regional criminal records check; preferably national criminal records check where applicable law permits.

- Education verification. Security officers should have at least a high school diploma or equivalent (GED).

• Pre-assignment screening should include, as a minimum:

- Possession of security guard or officer license where required by law.

- Completion of any state required security guard training requirements.

- Motor vehicle driver's record check if security is required to operate a company owned or leased vehicle.

- Citizenship verification if required by regulatory guidelines.

- Preferably, security officers should have at least 1 year security industry experience. However, this is sometimes difficult to achieve with the high turnover rate inherent to the contract security service industry.

- Supervisors should have 2 – 5 years security industry experience, with a minimum of 1 year experience in a supervisory capacity.

- Site security managers or supervisors responsible for overall onsite security services at the facility should have a minimum 3 – 5 years security supervision\management experience.

- Complex or regulated environments may dictate that security officers, supervisors and managers have direct industry related security experience prior to assignment.

• Pre-assignment training:

- A minimum of 4 (preferably 8 - 16) hours of training dedicated to general security roles and responsibilities.

- Successful completion of AED\CPR\First Aid training if the company requires security officers to be certified in AED\CPR\First Aid.

- Review and signing of the company's nondisclosure agreement for the site at which the security officer, supervisor or manager will be assigned to.

- On-the-Job Training (OJT)

The amount of OJT that a security officer or supervisor should receive is very subjective and is wholly dependent on the business environment, regulatory guidelines, position assignment and complexity\sensitivity of the position. The following are recommended minimum OJT training requirements.

- Security Officers and Receptionists: 24 to 40 hours of job specific training. Access control; visitor management; phone etiquette; patrol duties; vehicle operations, maintenance and service; incident response; review of security policy and procedure documents.

- Security Operations Center Officers: Completion of security officer OJT and a minimum of 16 – 24 hours training in electronic security systems monitoring, emergency response and notification procedures.

- Security Supervisors: Completion of security officer and security operations center officer OJT and a minimum of 8 hours training on supervisor specific duties and responsibilities.

- Security Managers: Although the site manager\supervisor may not work at a security post, they need to have a good understanding of the security program and the duties performed by the security staff they manage. Assuming the manager has a strong physical security background, training should be 24 – 40 hours on general security officer duties and responsibilities and the guiding principles of the business' physical security program.

- All assigned contract security staff should complete all contractor and site specific safety, business code of conduct and regulatory training requirements within required training windows.

Security Procedures

Security procedures provide detailed guidelines on the day-to-day operational aspects of the business' physical security program. The basic guidelines for security procedures are the same, whether you have a proprietary, contract or hybrid proprietary\contract security program. If you have a proprietary staff, they will normally develop the business' security procedures. Conversely, if your security is comprised solely of contract security personnel, the security services provider will normally develop the procedures; more commonly referred to as post orders. It is also not uncommon in mixed staffing structures for the proprietary staff to develop procedures for their duties and the security service provider to develop procedures for their duties.

Whenever relying on the contractor to develop site specific security procedures it is important that the documents be considered as a *client work product* and that clear language be included in the MSA that states that all documents identified as client work product remain the property of the client; not the contractor. It is not uncommon when transitioning from one security service provider to another that the outgoing contractor will take all of their post orders and blank forms with them; in turn leaving the contracting company and new contractor with the burden of developing new posts orders and forms. When site specific post orders and forms bear the contracting company's name (not the contractor's name) and they are designated as client work product, the outgoing contractor must leave them at the site when they transition out.

In either case, it is very important how the documents are titled; Standard Operating Procedures (SOP), Business Practice, Work Practice or Post Orders. In regulated environments, SOP's are considered to be regulated documents and all processes and procedures outlined in them must be validated, and they are subject to audit during any regulatory inspection. Any variances on the application of regulated SOP's must be documented with the type of variance, root cause of the variance and corrective actions taken to address the variance; all of which are also subject to regulatory audit. This is why security procedures documents in many pharmaceutical industry environments are referred to as business practices or work practices, which are usually not subject validation or regulatory audit.

For the purposes of this book, we will focus on security service provider post orders.

Most post orders across the contract security industry are boilerplate documents that are updated with site contact phone numbers and minor changes to address site specific security duties and responsibilities. The larger national and international security service provider post orders are usually more thorough and formatted better than smaller local providers' post orders are. However, the one thing they do have in common is that they normally contain excessive information that is not relevant to the actual functions of the security post, such as the contractor's company policies, the requirement to show up on time for work, disciplinary action process, etc. Although this is relevant information for the contractor's employees, it has nothing to do with the actual security functions of the post the security officer is assigned to. This information is better left to a separate policy manual that security officers and supervisors can refer to on an as needed basis.

When it comes to the actual procedures themselves, they are usually too wordy; explaining all of the idiosyncrasies related to the procedure before actually getting to the critical process steps of the procedure. This can be especially troublesome when it comes to emergency procedures where time is of the essence and process steps need to be clear and at the user's fingertips. If there is a fire, the security officer shouldn't have to thumb through pages of information on the causes of fire, fire prevention, fire extinguisher types and uses, and fire suppression system information before finally coming to the actual process steps somewhere on page 3 or 4. Yes, all of the information is useful to the security officer, but it should be in an operations\training manual separate from the post procedures manual.

Post security procedures need to be short, concise and to the point; detailing the procedural or process steps to be followed for routine security duties and emergency response. If a general statement needs to be added for clarity, it should be kept to no more than one paragraph and consist of 3 – 4 sentences at the beginning of the procedure.

Before moving forward with procedures recommendations it is important to note that in the absence of company security procedures, the post orders provided by the security provider are the business' accepted security procedures. Many security service providers request their client representative to sign off on the post orders they provide. Some clients sign them; many don't. Regardless of whether or not the service provider's post orders are signed by the client, once they are put in place there is implied acceptance of them as the business' security procedures as they were allowed to be posted and used. If for no other reason than this, security program managers should have input on the information contained in the procedures, review them for completeness and accuracy, and ensure any discrepancies or deficiencies are addressed before the procedures are posted for use.

There are two types of security procedures: routine procedures and emergency procedures. They should be kept in two separate color coded binders with labels indicating their content; red for emergency procedures and any other color you choose for day-to-day security operations procedures. The procedures should be indexed and have numbered section tabs, contain a table of contents with section and page numbers, a section on document change control, and include copies of all forms required in the procedures.

Security Operations Procedures

Security operations procedures outline the process steps to be followed for routine day-to-day security activities. They should address every type of activity that a security officer could reasonably be expected to encounter in the daily performance of their post duties. They can be general guidelines that apply to all posts, or tailored to meet post specific duties and responsibilities; such as receptionist procedures and loading dock procedures. If the procedure requires the completion of a form, then a copy of the form and the steps for completing it should be included. Much like a user manual, if the procedure requires the use of an application, such as a visitor management system, the process steps should be broken down with screenshots included for each step of the visitor registration process. If the procedure requires the checking or operation of equipment or systems, pictures of the relevant equipment or systems should also be included.

Although security procedures should be in line with established corporate security policy and standards, procedural guidelines will usually need to be adapted to the business unit or physical environment of a particular site. Security procedures for a company owned facility where the company is the sole tenant of the facility can focus on just company physical security protocols. However, if the company leases space within their facility, or is a tenant in leased space in a multitenant facility, security procedures will need to be adapted to incorporate tenant or landlord security requirements. The same holds true for different business units within the organization. A manufacturing facility or distribution center will have different site specific requirements than a corporate office building.

As a general rule, the following items should be included in the company's security procedures:

Access Control

The only way to limit access to company facilities is to require everyone entering the facility to present a valid company photo identification (ID) badge a lobby reception desk or at card reader controlled door. Anyone who does not have a valid company ID badge should be required to sign in and be escorted at all times while on company property. It is also very important that the access control policy\procedure be enforced uniformly across the organization. If exceptions are made for senior managers within an organization, line employees will see this and begin to question why they have to show or wear their badges and managers don't. It is also more common for managers who always wear their badge to require their employees to do the same; making security's job that much easier.

Consider the following when developing access control procedures:

- **Employees, Contractors and Vendors:** How will access be controlled for the workforce population? Will contractors and vendors have the same access as employees? Assuming contractors are nonemployees who work onsite on a regular basis and vendors are suppliers or service technicians who do not work on site on a regular basis, contractors should, for the most part, have the same access privileges as regular employees. Vendor access should be limited to normal business hours or hours to meet a specific business need; such as construction crews that may need after-hours access for building renovations, or service technicians that may require after-hours access to perform maintenance on building or infrastructure systems.

- **After-Hours Access:** Who will be allowed after-hours access to the facility? Should employees and contractors be required to sign in? This might be redundant if you have an access control system that is monitored by onsite security personnel.

  Should people coming in to work in the facility during after-hours times be required to check in with Security? This is a good idea when someone is working with hazardous materials (such as in a laboratory) or in a hazardous area (electrical room, mechanical room, etc.). Security can make periodic safety checks on the person(s) to ensure they are okay.

- **Visitor Access:** All visitors should be required to sign in and be escorted at all times by an authorized badge holder. All visitors 18 years of age and older should be required to show photo identification when signing in. Visitors should not be allowed after-hours access to the facility without prior approval of a management level employee of the company. If the company or one of its employees will be hosting a meeting or event, how will non-employee attendee access be handled? How will access be handled for event catering staff? If the site is subject to regulatory audit, how will regulatory inspectors be handled when they arrive on site? Can visitors be preregistered? If yes, what it the process for preregistering guests?

  It is also important to put in provisions for legal process service. This should be coordinated with the company's legal department for company related process services and human resources for personal process services (attachment of wages, summons, subpoena, warrant). Whenever possible law enforcement, unless in the pursuit of a fleeing person, should not be allowed to enter the facility to question someone on the property without first coordinating with the legal and human resources department. Advance coordination with law enforcement on developing appropriate procedures for onsite interviews will go a long way in developing good company\law enforcement relations, while at the same time working to ensure employee workplace privacy rights.

- **Restricted Area Access:** Restricted areas can be defined as any areas within a facility that require enhanced security measures to provide for the protection of critical infrastructure, proprietary or confidential information, critical business processes and workplace safety. These include, but are not limited to, research & development laboratories, manufacturing floors, hazardous material storage areas, data centers and distribution fields, mechanical and electrical rooms, and legal, quality assurance\control, customer and human resources files. The procedures put in place for restricted area access should include:

  - Appointment of restricted area access approvers with minimum semiannual reviews.

  - Access request and approval process.

  - Process for adding and removing access.

- When access should be removed (i.e., Person terminates employment or is reassigned to another position and they no longer require access as part of their daily job functions.)

- Regular periodic reviews of all restricted area cardholder reports.

- The process for issuing keys if a card reader controlled door stops working and a temporary key needs to be issued for access.

- Many organizations have an "All Doors" 24 x 7 access level that is issued to select personnel within an organization. Managers should restrict this access level to only those personnel, such as facilities, safety and security personnel who may require access as a part of their daily job functions. This should not be a default access granted to senior management personnel who do not have a business need for access to these areas on a daily basis. (i.e., The CEO does not require access to the data center or critical infrastructure areas to perform their job.)

- **Badge Issue and Control:** How will company badges be issued to employees, contractors and vendors? What doors will be included in the "General" access level given to all onsite personnel and what will the hours of access be? What is the process for forgotten, lost or stolen badges? Who will be responsible for collecting badges from terminated personnel? (Manager, HR, Security?) How will short notice terminations for cause be handled?

- **Emergency Services Access:** Every access control policy\procedure should contain a statement that reads… *"This policy (procedure) does not apply to emergency services personnel (police, fire department, emergency medical services) responding to actual emergency conditionals in the facility."* This provision allows for emergency access to the site and its restricted areas without responders having to be signed in. This is important when working in regulatory environments. It will help to alleviate the question of why emergency services personnel didn't sign in when they came into the facility. It may sound a bit crazy, but this question has been raised during regulatory audits.

Property Control

Property control poses its own special set of concerns across many industries. Some organizations implement property control procedures while others don't.

The biggest concern for most organizations is *theft of company property –v– corporate culture.* We want to protect our assets, but we don't want to inconvenience our employees. For this reason, the best approach for determining property control guidelines is a risk management approach. While it is not customary for people leaving the building with laptop bags containing company laptops and information, there should be procedures in place for removing company tools and equipment. If someone is removing a server, desktop computer, monitors or other equipment, they should have written approval from their manager or the person responsible for the equipment.

The easiest and most effective form of property control is the property pass system. Property passes are issued to track and monitor property taken out of and at times brought into a facility. Property passes should contain the person's name, company, department, date, time and an itemized description (including serial numbers) of property being hand-carried out of the facility. The person removing the property should also be required to have a valid company ID badge. This system works very well and if done properly will not unduly inconvenience employees, contractors or vendors.

Consideration also needs to be given to deliveries and equipment being brought into the facility. Restrictions should be placed on the types of items that can be brought into a facility through building lobby doors (flower & takeout food deliveries, small packages, etc.) and which items should be brought in through the loading dock (large equipment, large packages, hazardous materials, etc.).

If the site is a manufacturing or processing facility, procedures should be put in place for the handling, storage and removal of high value scrap materials; such as copper and other high value metal shavings and plugs. If the facility has high value scrap materials as a result of the production process, consideration should be given to the placement of scrap bins (do not place them near building perimeter doors), securing the bins and removal of materials by the authorized scrap metal collection company.

Lastly, it is always good to place a sign at all lobby desks that reads *"All hand-carried items being brought into or taken out of this facility are subject to security inspection at any time."* It is important to use the word "inspection" as opposed to "search". A search, by definition is more intrusive than an inspection and people subconsciously take less offense to their bag or package being inspected as opposed to searched.

Security Patrols

Security patrols provide a visible deterrent to illegal activities as well as provide a means of checking for building system abnormalities and water and other fluid leaks. Outline what security officers are expected to check during their patrols, how often patrols should be conducted and the reporting procedures for deficiencies or deviances noted during routine patrols.

Building Opening and Closing

Describe when and how the building should be opened and closed at the beginning and end of each business day. If elevators must be turned on or off, or doors need to be unlocked or locked, describe the steps required for each of these tasks.

Security Systems Monitoring

An electronic physical security system that is not monitored by trained security personnel provides no real-time protection to a company and serves no other purpose than as a tool for granting badge access and incident\event follow up investigations. Identify alarm types and the actions to be taken whenever an alarm is activated. Outline daily and periodic systems checks and the process to follow when a system error or malfunction is identified.

Building Management Systems Monitoring

If security is responsible for monitoring building systems (HVAC, fire alarm, electrical, lab equipment, etc.), procedures outlining the systems monitoring and response procedures for system alarms and failures should be developed.

Other Duties

If security is responsible for any other duties not previously discussed, it is imperative that written procedures be developed for these duties. When considering what other duties security should or can take on, managers need to consider the impact of *nontraditional security duties* on the security function. While some additional duties make sense and align with overall safety and security objectives, such as having visitors complete a safety briefing, others such as having employees call in to security when they call off for work or are running late, or having security issue employee paychecks do not contribute to workplace safety and security and can actually detract from the security mission.

Emergency Procedures

It goes without saying that security is an integral part of a company or facility's emergency response plans. Security is usually responsible for initiating response to fire alarms, medical emergencies, power outages and hazardous material spills, to name just a few. As part of these duties, security is also responsible for making appropriate notifications to outside emergency response agencies and company representatives responsible for event specific emergency response activities. Depending on the nature and extent of the emergency, security response protocols can range from basic incident identification and notification to complex situational analysis and response steps. Response to a chemical leak\spill with personal contamination will inherently be more complex than response to a power surge or failure.

When developing security emergency procedures:

- Identify the extent of security's role in incident response,
- Identify emergency event priorities (low, medium, high),
- Identify response protocols to meet each event type, and
- Develop concise procedures that are easy to read and follow.

Two of the biggest areas of concern with most security emergency procedures are that they are usually too wordy and\or do not contain comprehensive checklists for gathering emergency incident information. This is especially true for most, but not all, contract security provider emergency procedures. As an example, most fire alarm emergency procedures will start out with section on fire hazards, the fire triangle, types of fires and fire extinguishers, security's role and then somewhere on page 3 it says... Call 911 and initiate emergency evacuation. When an emergency or disaster strikes, time is of the essence and depending on the nature of the incident, lives and serious property damage could hang in the balance. Every minute the security officer spends looking for emergency response steps is another minute that passes by before emergency response actions can be initiated.

When developing emergency procedures it is best to use a bullet point or flowchart format with an accompanying checklist that contains all information that should be collected on the incident and the contact names and phone numbers of the people to be notified in the event an emergency arises. This is especially true for complex incidents that require the security officer to analyze the situation and then take specific steps based on the nature of the incident. A perfect example of this is a hazardous material leak\spill. An equipment fluid leak, natural gas leak or toxic chemical spill will require different response protocols. The same can be said if there is personnel contamination involved. When security receives a call or identifies a hazardous material leak\spill, they must first determine the type of material involved, the extent of the leak\spill and any personnel contamination before making the appropriate notification. A sample Hazmat Leak\Spill flowchart procedure and accompanying checklist are provided on pages 50 & 51 for reference. The decision making tree and checklist provide the security officer with all of the information they require to initiate response on two pages. The checklist can be removed and attached to a separate incident report to document incident identification and initial response efforts.

As a minimum, the following types of incidents should be considered for inclusion in security's emergency response procedures:

- Fire Alarm
- Fire
- Medical (Injury\Illness)
- Hazardous Material Leak\Spill
- Power Outage\Surge
- Water Leak
- Elevator Entrapment (if applicable)
- Severe Weather
- Bomb Threat
- Suspicious Items\Packages
- Threats
- Activist\Protest Activities
- Building Intruder
- Restraining\Protective Order Violations
- Active Shooter

Lastly, managers need to take into consideration what security is and is not capable of doing. Any incident that requires security to participate in direct response efforts, such as applying first aid or containing a hazardous material spill will require the security officer to have certifiable training in those procedures.

Anyone physically responsible for responding to a medical emergency should be required to obtain certification in AED\CPR\First Aid. Similarly, if a security officer is required to use a spill kit to contain a spill\leak, they should be trained in the use of the kit and any appropriate personal protective equipment (PPE) they must wear. Consideration also needs to be given to how many people, based on the procedures written, it will take to effectively accomplish the task at hand. A fire alarm response procedure that requires a security officer to make immediate notifications, investigate the alarm, conduct a floor sweep for evacuation purposes, escort firefighters to the alarm location and not allow anyone to enter the building until the fire department gives the all clear cannot be accomplished if there is only one security officer on duty. Wherever possible, emergency procedures should include cross-functional duties that can\will be performed by non-security personnel who can also effectively respond to the incident.

HAZARDOUS MATERIAL LEAK\SPILL

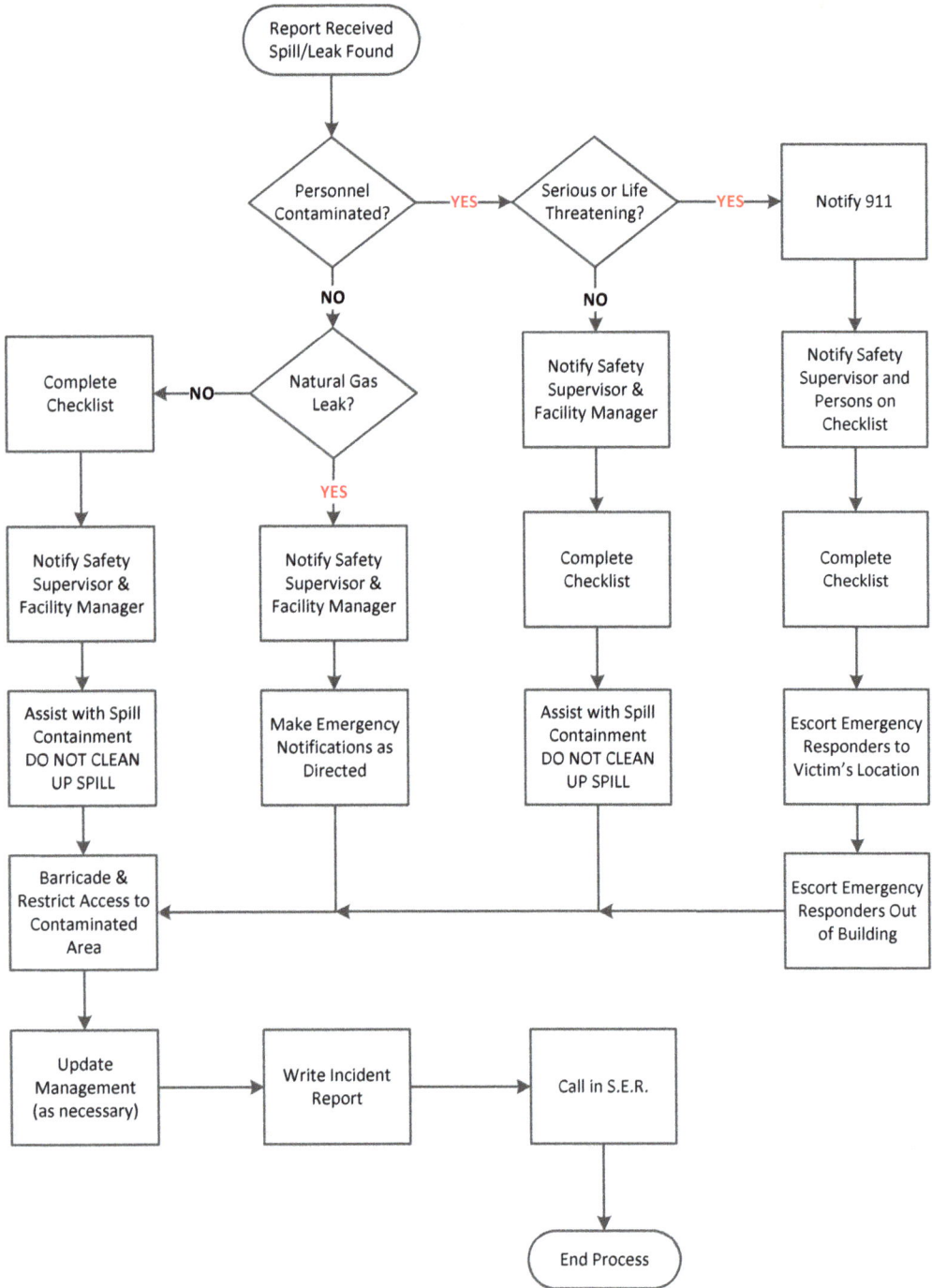

Figure 4: Hazmat Spill\Leak Flow Chart

HAZARDOUS MATERIAL SPILL\LEAK

Date:	**Time:**
Caller's Name:	**Callback Number:**

Location: Bldg: Floor: Area\Room Name or #:

Is anyone Injured: ☐ Yes – Initial Medical Emergency Response Procedures ☐ No

Material Type: ☐ Biological ☐ Chemical ☐ Radiological
Material Name:

Material Charaacteristics: ☐ Liquid ☐ Solid ☐ Vapor ☐ Thick ☐ Runny Color:

NFPA Label Information: ◆ ◆ ◆ ◇

Other Hazard Label: ☐ Toxic ☐ Poison ☐ Corrosive ☐ Acid ☐ Other:

Approximate amount \ area covered?

Has spill been contained? ☐ Yes (spill kit?) ☐ No **Is it spreading?** ☐ Yes ☐ No

What was the source of the spill \ leak?
☐ Equipment ☐ Container\Barrel ☐ Cabinet ☐ Vehicle ☐ Other:

Has area been barricaded? ☐ Yes (go to next) ☐ No (restrict access to area)

IMMEDIATE NOTIFICATIONS		
Facilities Notification (Name)	Time Notified	Callback Time\Comments
Safety Notification (Name)	Time Notified	Callback Time\Comments
Security Notification (Name)	Time Notified	Callback Time\Comments

ESCALATION NOTIFICATIONS – ONLY AS DIRECTED		
Fire Department	Time Notified	Time on Scene
Ambulance\Hospital	Time Notified	Callback Time\Comments
Other (Name)	Time Notified	Callback Time\Comments
Other (Name)	Time Notified	Callback Time\Comments

Chapter 5

Electronic Physical Security Systems

Electronic physical security systems (EPSS) consist of two primary elements: Access Control Systems (ACS) and Video Management Systems (VMS). When properly installed, integrated and maintained, EPSS provide an organization with an effective means for delaying entering to facilities and assets, detecting unauthorized entry\illicit activities and responding to intrusions and suspicious activities. Although there is a plethora of ACS and VMS platforms a company can choose from to meet the security needs their of organization, there are some common aspects that apply to most systems when it comes to network architecture, operating environment and systems configuration. This chapter addresses the commonalities across various platforms.

System Architecture

System architecture is concerned with the network infrastructure and servers required to support the system. Bandwidth, server and switch requirements can vary significantly depending on the EPPS's component parts and system size. Understanding these variables and what they mean in information technology (IT) capital and expense budgets and support requirements will assist managers in designing systems that operate effectively and efficiently with the company's IT support capabilities. In addition to *"production"* servers, organizations should also include back-up EPSS servers in their business resiliency plans to assure continuity of security operations. Most systems can operate in a virtual environment. Some platforms are also compatible with Wi-Fi and Cloud technology.

For system architectural design purposes in this handbook, network infrastructure is broken down into two categories: enterprise network architecture and distributed network architecture.

Access Control System Architecture

Enterprise Network Architecture

This network architecture assumes that:

- There is one primary and one backup ACS application and database server deployed.

  - Many ACS applications have internal databases that do not require an external database server.

  - If the ACS application is integrated with the Human Resource Management System (HRMS) and personnel data is drawn from the HRMS database to populate cardholder personnel records, integration is usually accomplished through a Lightweight Directory Access Protocol (LDAP) feed.

- The application is used to control access to one or more facilities across the enterprise.

- The system can be administered and monitored by a single central station or sites may administer and monitor their respective systems individually.

- The central station always has the capability to administer and monitor all sites, regardless of whether or not a site performs these tasks themselves.

The ACS network architecture pictured in Figure 5 will work well for most small to medium size organizations on both a local and regional basis. The number of sites, doors, card readers, inputs, outputs and cardholder records that can be added to the system are only limited by the application and database. Additions and changes made at any system workstation can populate the databases without each site having to make individual changes, if desired. If a person's employment is voluntarily or involuntarily terminated, removal of cardholder access to all sites can be accomplished from one workstation. Sites can also act as backups to each other.

Although this is a reasonable solution for small and medium size organizations, it is not a good model for large national or global organizations. The issue with this model in large companies is that it allows for a single point of failure across the entire organization. If there is a network failure at the headend or the system crashes, all sites will be affected simultaneously. This could also happen during IT maintenance windows where the network or servers are temporarily taken down for upgrades. Although individual site information such as site access privileges, devices and alarm data are stored locally in the security system panels and people will still have regular access to their worksites, nothing can be done with the system while it is down. No personnel records can be added or changed, and alarms cannot be monitored as there is no connection between system servers, security panels or system administration and monitoring stations. Additionally, when the system comes back on line, all of the alarm data stored in the security panels at all sites will be sent to the system's primary and backup servers. Depending of the duration of the outage, size of the system and alarm programming conventions, the volume of alarms coming in could also cause the system to crash.

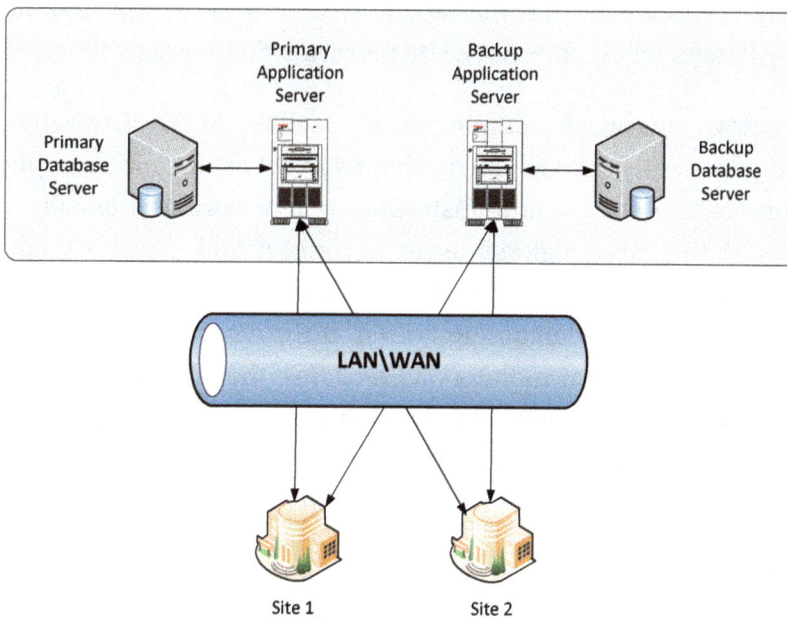

Figure 5: Access Control System Enterprise Network Architecture

Large organizations should consider distributed network architecture for their ACS. This type of network architecture allows for regional control, eliminates the likelihood of a single point of failure and facilitates business continuity. If the headend goes down, each region can still operate independently. If a regional server goes down, the site systems in those regions can still be administered and monitored from the headend or another region.

Distributed Network Architecture

A distributed ACS network architecture assumes that:

- There is one primary and one backup ACS application and database headend server.

- Facilities located throughout the organization are grouped into regions (i.e. US-East, US-West, Europe, India, etc.)

- All systems operate on a common enterprise network.

- Individual sites can be administered and monitored on a local, regional or global basis.

- The headend always has the capability to administer and monitor all sites, regardless of whether or not a site performs these tasks themselves.

Figure 6 below shows a simple three region ACS distributed network configuration. Under this model the headend servers as the master application and database servers. No system administration or monitoring is usually done from these servers. Rather, site\regional users administer and monitor their respective systems. Any changes they make at their sites are stored on their database server(s) and the headend database server(s). If the company has a global security operations center (SOC) that monitors all facilities, the SOC may use the headend server for monitoring all sites. Application programming can also be set to automatically transfer site system monitoring from one site to another. This is discussed in more detail in the section on *Software Platforms.*

As with the standard enterprise network configuration, the number of regions, sites, doors, card readers, inputs, outputs and cardholder records that can be added to the system are only limited by the application and database size.

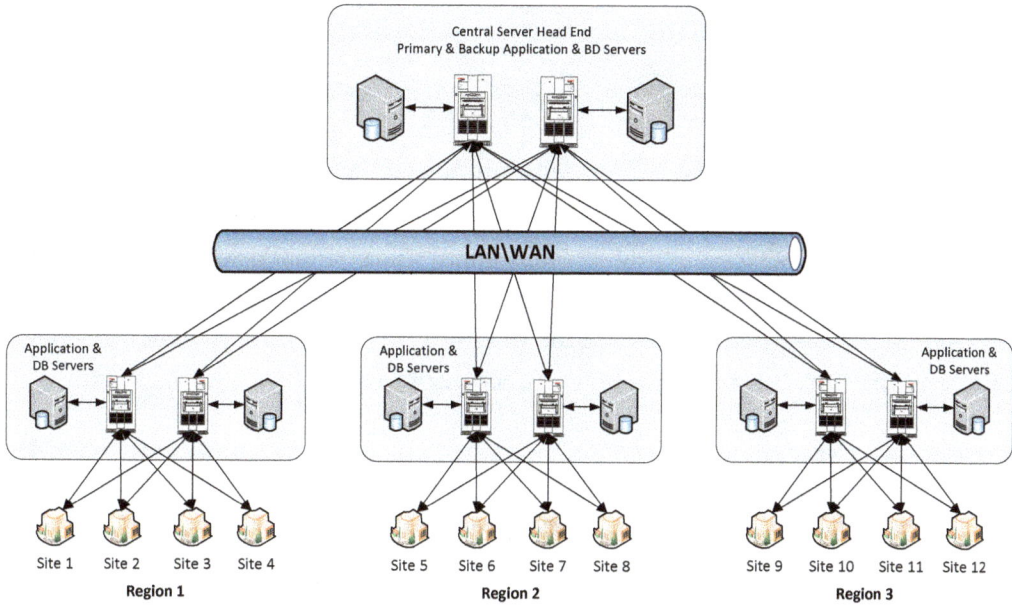

Figure 6: Access Control System Distributed Network Architecture

The key advantages of the distributed network configuration are:

- There is no single point of failure. If the headend servers or network go down, all regional platforms will continue to operate seamlessly. Similarly, if a region goes down, the headend and all other regions will continue to operate seamlessly.

- In additional to backup database servers at the regional level, all regional databases are backed up to the headend database(s). In the event of a catastrophic regional system failure, the regional database can be restored from the headend database.

- Increases business resiliency by allowing multiple regions to act as backup security operations centers. With standard application programming, designated user profiles can be configured to allow for complete or partial takeover of designated sites across one or more regions. If a site has to be evacuated for whatever reason, designated users can take over all administration and monitoring for the affected site until normal operations can be resumed.

Facility Level ACS Architecture

As the previous two sections focused on network infrastructure design considerations for the ACS application platform, this section focuses on the basic concepts of site level system component requirements. As the type and number of system component parts such as panels and modules can vary significantly from one platform to another, it would be impossible to list every possible configuration without devoting an entire book to it. That being the case, the concepts outlined in this section are designed to provide the reader with enough high level information to understand how a typical site level ACS is configured.

Generally speaking, facility level ACS architecture is similar to that of most BMS systems that operate on the facility's LAN\WAN and has headend server(s), control panels, inputs and outputs, as well as power supplies for electric doors locks. Figure 7 below shows a simple network architecture for an ACS with two security control panels. Adding more panels to the system would normally require nothing more than running additional RJ45 network cable for the panels, obtaining a network ID address, and adding an additional switch\hub, as necessary.

Security Control Panels (Controllers)

Security control panels act as the interface between the ACS system servers and the card readers, inputs and outputs installed throughout the facility. Each panel comes with a motherboard, card reader ports, input and output boards, a network communications board, a low voltage power supply (12v or 24v DC) that provides power to card readers, inputs and outputs, and a backup battery power supply (4-hours). Some panels also have the capability to provide power of Ethernet (PoE) to devices connected to the panel. All panels require an AC power supply (110v 220v) and a network connection (hardwired or WiFi).

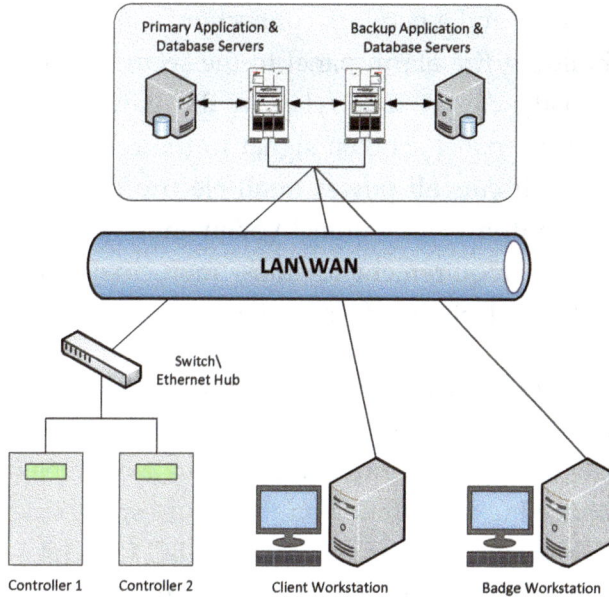

Figure 7: ACS Control Panel Architecture

As with any BMS system, the ACS should be connected to the facility's UPS and\or emergency generator circuits. If it is not and power to the panel is lost and the backup battery power runs out, all card access controlled doors will no longer work, inputs and outputs will not work, no data can be uploaded to or transmitted from the panel and, in extreme cases, the panel may need to be restored from the application database once power is restored. This is also why it is important for any door lock power supplies to be on the facility's emergency power system. Normally fail safe electric door locks, where power loss to the lock will cause the door to automatically unlock or release, will also unlock during a power outage if the power supply is not connected to the building UPS\emergency generator circuit.

Most security panels come in 2, 4, 8 and 16 door configurations. There are some rack mounted controllers on the market that can support as many 32 doors. The standard number of inputs, outputs and card readers a controller can support is usually in direct proportion to the number of doors the panel is configured for. There is normally 1 reader port and 2 input and 2 output ports for each door. Thus, if you have an 8 door panel, there will normally be 8 card reader ports, 16 input ports and 16 output ports. Expansion modules (boards) for additional readers, inputs and outputs can be purchased to increase panel capacity. The only limiting factor is the size of the panel box itself.

In addition to AC power and a network connection, a *dry contact* line also needs to be run from the building fire alarm panel to the security control panel. This line connects to a normally closed lock relay in the panel. When a fire alarm is activated, the fire alarm panel sends a signal to the relay that causes it to open. When the relay opens it cuts all power to all electric doors locks; causing doors with fail safe locks to automatically unlock\open on fire alarm activation. This is a standard building code requirement for most municipalities for electromagnetic locks or any other electric lock that does not have a mechanical key override.

Although there are many different door configurations, the typical configurations depicted in figures 8 & 9 can be used for most doors with only slight modifications for door type and locking hardware. If using an electromagnetic lock, a door release button will need to be installed on the secure space side of the door to cut power to the lock in the event of an emergency (IBC 1008.1.4.4 Access-Controlled Egress Doors). If using an electric lock with a request to exit (RTE) device in the handle, an RTE above door will not be required.

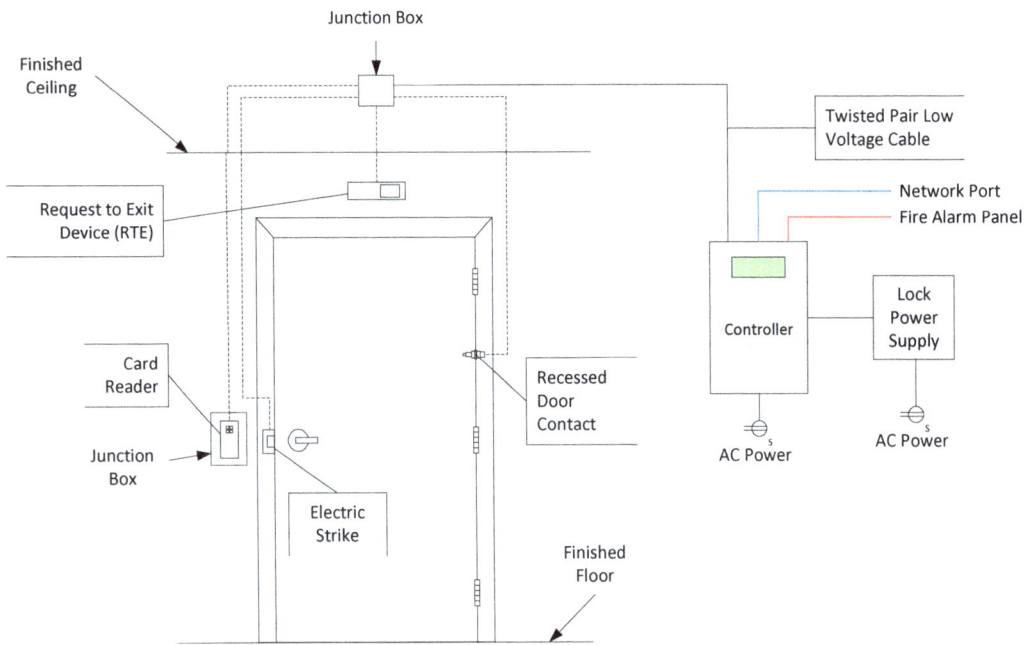

Figure 8: Typical Single Door Configuration – Electric Strike

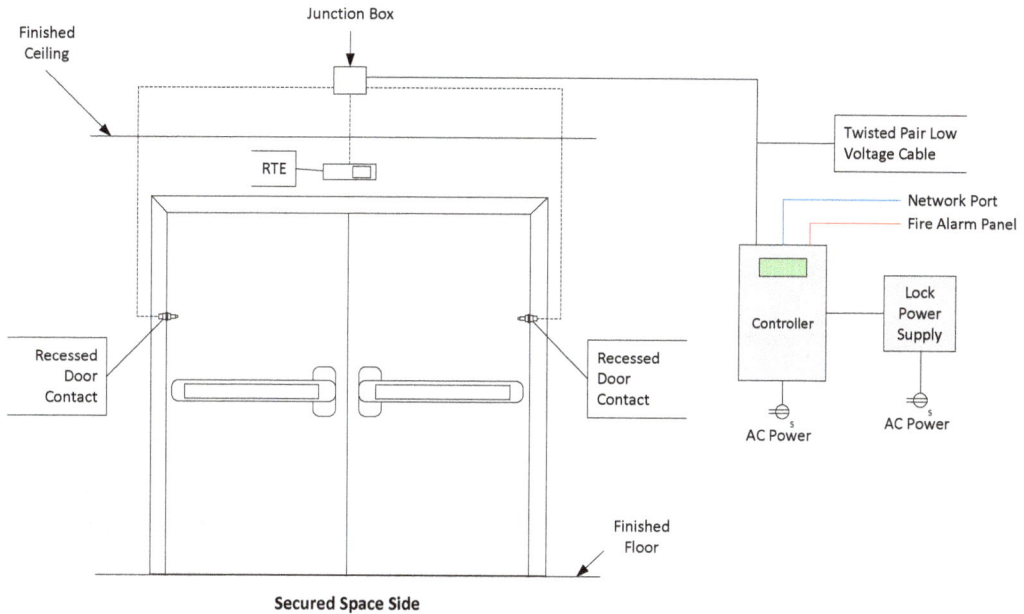

Junction Box

Finished
Ceiling

RTE

Twisted Pair Low
Voltage Cable

Network Port
Fire Alarm Panel

Lock
Power
Supply

Controller

Recessed
Door
Contact

Recessed
Door
Contact

AC Power

AC Power

Finished
Floor

Secured Space Side

Figure 9: Typical Exit Only Double Door without Electric Lock\Strike

As a general rule, ACS device wiring should be home-run from the device to the controller. Additionally, the ACS should be a supervised system. It is all too often that ACS's are installed as non-supervised systems. The end result is a system where a device may fail or communication with a device may be lost due to a wire inadvertently or maliciously being cut, with system monitoring personnel not knowing about the issue until a) it is found during regular system maintenance, b) someone complains about a door not working properly or c) an unauthorized person gains access to the building or a restricted area. Installing end-of-line resistors at devices and activating the supervised input\output feature in the ACS application will notify system monitors of any communication issues with devices. This facilitates proactive rather than reactive system maintenance.

As more businesses transition to smart building technology it is important to note that most commercial ACS platforms have the capability to integrate seamlessly with other building management system platforms and controllers. To accomplish this, the ACS and BMS need to be compatible and fully integrated. From there it is just a matter of system programming and adding input\output boards to the ACS, as necessary, to meet the smart building design concept.

Video Management System Architecture

There are two basic types of CCTV cameras: Analog cameras and IP cameras. The type of cameras chosen will dictate the systems architecture and network components the system will require. With the advancements made in IP camera technology and analog cameras slowly being phased out, with some no longer being supported, managers should look to upgrade from analog to IP based VMS platforms.

Typical analog camera architecture (Figure 10 below) is basic and does not require a significant amount of network\fiber optic cabling. A network connection is required between the digital video recorder (DVR), storage server and client\monitoring workstations. Cameras are connected to the DVR through coax cable home-run from the cameras to the DVR. An external power supply is also required to provide power to the cameras.

IP CCTV cameras inherently consume large amounts of bandwidth when transmitting live video feeds. It is for this reason that most VMS network architecture is configured at the site level as opposed to distributed network architecture. Each site should have its own local network architecture and VMS servers, with only a limited number of *critical cameras* monitored on a continual basis. Video footage also consumes a large amount of server storage space, which has led to the benchmark standard of setting cameras to record on motion only. More is discussed about this in the section on system platforms and system monitoring. VMS video storage servers should have a minimum 1 terabyte storage capacity or more, depending on minimum video retention times and the number of cameras at any given facility.

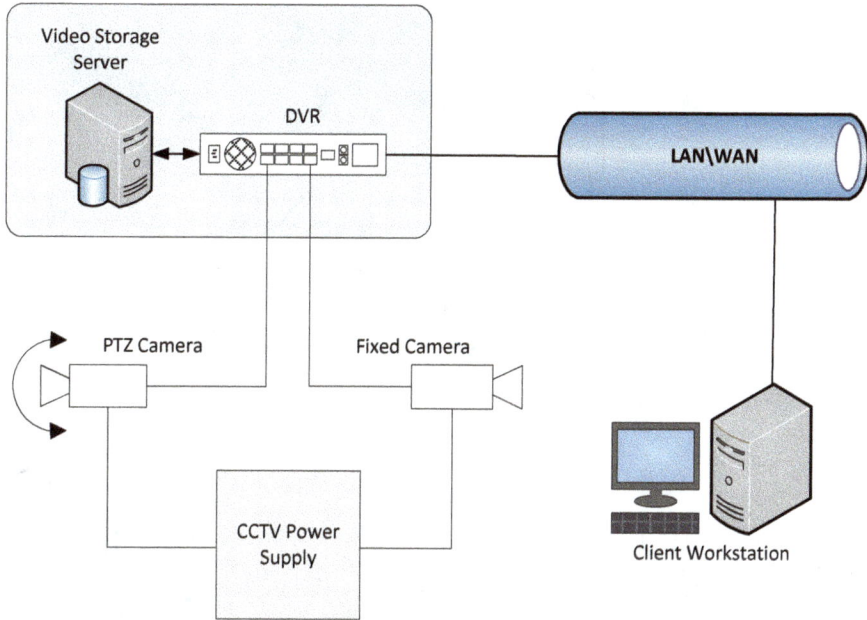

Figure 10: Typical Analog CCTV Camera Architecture

IP camera system architecture can vary significantly based on the type of network video server (NVR) and the types of cameras connected to the system. Newer NVRs have the capability to provide power over Ethernet (PoE), while older NVRs require a separate PoE switch. In addition to IP cameras, analog cameras can also be connected to an NVR. This requires the addition of a digital converter between the analog camera and the Ethernet switch. There are also power over coax (PoC) adapters available that can provide camera power from an NVR or PoE switch to analog cameras. This is a good option for organizations considering conversion form existing analog based VMS platforms to IP based systems.

Figure 11 below shows a typical IP camera architecture with both an IP and analog camera. If the NVR has PoE capability, only an Ethernet\network switch will be required for connection between the cameras and the NVR. Similarly, if a PoC adapter is used for analog camera power supply, the adapter should be installed between the digital converter and NVR\PoE switch.

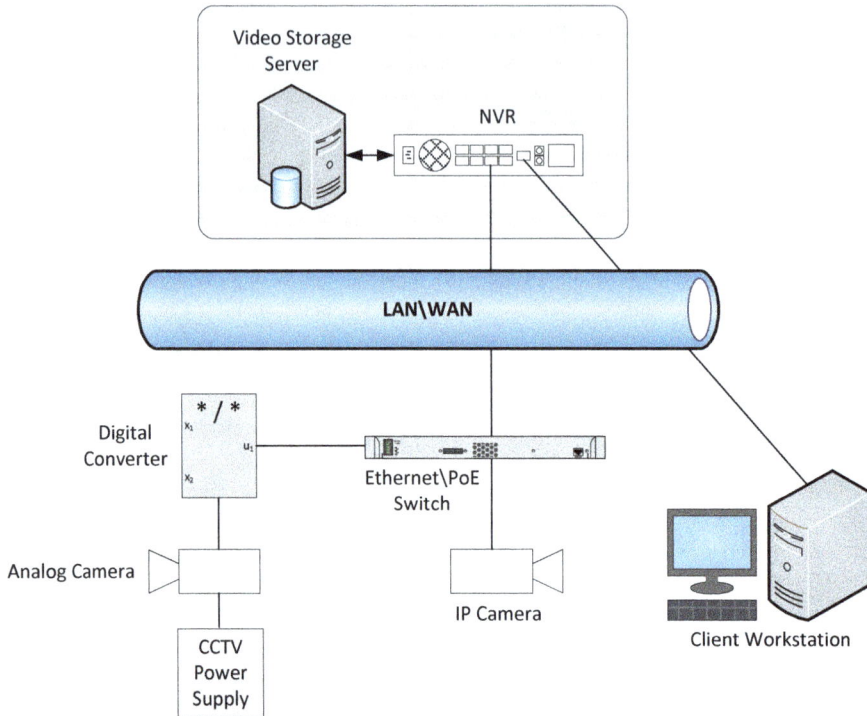

Figure 11: Typical IP CCTV Camera Architecture

ACS & VMS Software Platforms

The platforms selected should be commercial grade and be approved by the company's IT department. A software support agreement (SSA) for all applications should also be purchased for all installed systems. The SSA allows for regular application updates and facilitates system technical support. Systems designed for private home use simply do not have the capacity to meet the demands of the commercial business environment. They have very limited features, are not suited for card access functions and cannot be integrated with other security or business applications.

When selecting an application platform, organizations should strongly consider platforms with an open architecture that allow the application to integrate with other applications as opposed to closed proprietary applications. In closed proprietary systems, the manufacturer usually restricts what other systems can integrate with their system. In almost all cases, this means that the system owner can only purchase the manufacturer's applications, servers and components; or the applications, servers and components of 1 or 2 of the manufacture's business partners. This can severely limit the system owner's ability to purchase newer, more robust technology that could better meet the security needs of the business.

It is also not uncommon that closed systems are not compatible with most integration software applications that facilitate systems integration across multiple\divergent applications. As such, closed systems also end up costing more in the long run as market competition is restricted and the system owner may need to replace their entire system in order to achieve a more robust system or migrate to smart building technology.

When a company acquires or leases new facilities or space, they should make plans for migrating the new site's EPSS to the company's preferred platforms. Not doing so can leave a company with divergent systems that are not compatible with each other. If the company has a central security operation center (SOC) which monitors all company facilities, this could result in the requirement of additional capital equipment to facilitate systems monitoring. It could also lead missed alarms and events as SOC operators have to monitor two or more systems simultaneously.

Another concern when dealing with leased space in a multitenant facility is that site security access control remains with the landlord, not the company leasing the space. If employees or contractors are hired or terminated, the tenant must contact the landlord to have them added to or removed the building's access control system. Sometimes this can take more than 24-hours to accomplish. In the event of an emergency last minute termination, this could result in a terminated person having access to the site until the landlord effects badge access termination. As there is no control over the landlords' badge issue and control program, there is also the possibility that a former tenant may still have access to the space after it is occupied by another tenant.

The relatively small investment required for a company to install their own card reads, door devices and CCTV cameras will ensure access to the space is controlled in accordance with company security guidelines. Adding and removing card access to the space can be done from a central location and the company's security department can monitor the space and initiate alarm\incident response protocols in accordance with company security procedures.

Systems Programming & Integration

The very first thing to do after installing any system platform software is to change the manufacture's default Admin username and password. Default Admin accounts and passwords are set to make it easier for manufacturer certified technicians to log in as System Administrators (SysAdmin) to program and make changes to the system. Most of these default usernames\passwords are usually very simple, such as Admin\Admin, Admin\Password, Admin\12345. There are even some with no username or password. Although this may work well for system integrator technicians, it is bad IT security protocol. If you were to put down this book right now, open up your internet web browser and type "default password" and your system name in the search bar, chances are your search will come back with a link that will provide you with the default username and password for the system. If it's that easy for you to do, a hacker will have no problem obtaining the same Admin username and password. Usernames and passwords should be set for each integrator technician working on the system and be in line with the company's IT security guidelines.

At no time should the SysAdmin user privilege be the default privilege assigned to all system users. The SysAdmin privilege should also not be assigned to a person based solely on their position title; the facility manager should not be assigned the SysAdmin privilege just because they are the facility manager. Neither should there be a default username and password for system users. Individual user profiles should be set for all systems users.

- SysAdmin: Integrator technicians and 2 – 3 designated SysAdmins who have received either manufacturer or company designed\approved SysAdmin training on the system(s).

- System User: Persons who log on to and monitor the system on a daily basis. User privileges may be tiered to allow for expanded privileges based on the person's job title\responsibilities. Expanded privileges could be set for cardholder profile creation, badge deactivation, manual door unlocks and facility lockdown events.

Naming Conventions

As previously discussed in Facility Security Standards, companies should use standard naming conventions when programming their ACS and VMS systems.

Standard naming conventions make easier to identify system components and their links, as well as make it easier for system programming, integration, monitoring and troubleshooting. An effective naming convention is to set a name for all system components, alarms, actions and access levels that includes the building number, floor and room number and name. As most Facilities departments assign facility or property numbers to all buildings and properties, these numbers may be incorporated in the systems' naming convention. This will make it easier for cross-referencing systems with specific properties, tracking total building operating costs and make migration to smart building technology easier.

A standard naming convent for a company with global properties might look something like this:

Facility # – Country – City – Street – Address

2525-US- PHX-35 Papago = 35 Papago St., Phoenix, AZ, USA

3752-GE-BLN-2633 Hauptmann = 2633 Hauptmann Strasse, Berlin, Germany

A standard naming convent for a company with national properties might look something like this:

Facility # – State\Provence – City – Street – Address

1836-MA-BOS-97 Beacon = 97 Beacon St., Boston, MA

5004-IN-IND-1900 Meridian = 1900 Meridian St., Indianapolis, IN

The complete name may be used for naming servers, controllers, components and CCTV cameras while a condensed name may be used for access clearance names and alarm messages.

State\Provence – City – Address – Clearance Name

MA-BOS-97 Beacon – General

General access clearance for people working at 97 Beacon St.

State\Provence – City – Address – Room Name, Floor -Room Number – Alarm

MA-BOS-97 Beacon – Hazmat Storage Rm 3-3725 – Held

The door to hazmat storage room #3725 on the 3rd floor of 97 Beacon St. is being held open.

State\Provence – City – Address – CCTV Camera Name

MA-BOS-97 Beacon–LD (05)

CCTV camera #05, 97 Beacon St. Loading Dock.

Regardless of the naming convention used, whether similar to the examples provided or something different, it should be consistent across all facilities and EPSS installed at those facilities. Prior to installing a new system or adding to an existing system, the system integrator should be provided with the approved system naming conventions for the project.

Access Control System

There are four primary components to ACS programming that security program managers should become familiar with: *access levels, events, manual actions and system integration.*

Access Levels

Access levels should mirror the layered facility protection model discussed in Chapter 2, Physical Security Concepts: *controlled, limited and restricted areas.* Access to the controlled and limited areas can be included in the *general* access level assigned to the general workforce population. Organizations may wish to further define general access levels for employees, contractors and vendors, such as restrictions on hours of access; employees may receive 24 x 7 access while contractors receive Monday – Friday, business hours access. General access can be specific to one building or a group of buildings, which is common practice in campus environments or companies with facilities in multiple regions. As a general rule though, each facility\campus should have a general access level that applies to that facility\campus and that is assigned to only those people who have a business need to be at the site on a daily basis. Access to other campuses or facilities should be on an as needed\requested basis.

Restricted area access levels should be programmed for areas defined as restricted areas within a facility. Access to these areas should only be added to person's access card after approval from an authorized approver for the area is received. At no time should any restricted area doors be included in the general access level.

Another access level is the *all doors* clearance that allows a cardholder unrestricted 24 x 7 access to all doors at a facility or within the access control system. This clearance should only be assigned to emergency service agency access cards (fire department) or critical support personnel (facility technicians, safety personnel, etc.) who have completed all training and background requirements for access to each restricted area. A common mistake made by many organizations is to automatically assign the all doors clearance as the default access for senior executives. The argument most often used in support this practice is that C-Level employees are responsible for management of all company functions, therefore they should have unrestricted access to all areas. This line of reasoning is not only irrational, but it can also lead to regulatory violations in any regulated industry. A question that should be asked by all mangers is: *Why does the CEO, CFO, CIO or any other senior executive require 24 x 7 access to building infrastructure areas, hazardous material storage areas, data centers or any other sensitive areas within a facility?* In a regulated environment, it will be much easier to explain to a senior executive why they don't have access, as opposed to explaining why their access was removed as the result of a deviation or discrepancy noted during a regulatory or certification audit.

Events

Events are merely the actions that a system performs as the result of an input or output being triggered. Examples of these are card reads at a door. A valid card read allows the person access through a door; pressing a door release button unlocks a door for a specified period of time; an alarmed door that is opened with a key or held open more than a designated period of time will trigger a door forced\held alarm; doors are programmed to lock and unlock at specified times on certain days of the week. These are all standard programming requirements for ACS and are performed by all system integrators during system installation and upgrades. However, the area of most concern for event programming is event messaging.

Most integrators program all event messages to be logged in the system journal *and* show up at the monitoring station. This means that every event in the system will show up on the monitoring screen; every card read, every time a door opens or closes, every time the system backs itself up; literally everything. Integrators say this is done so system monitoring personnel can monitor everything that is taking place in the system, thereby allowing them to identify issues and effectively respond to them. Nothing could be further from the truth. When ACS event messaging is programmed in this manner, event messaging on the monitoring station screen constantly scrolls through every event as it is triggered. The amount of data scrolling on the screen can be so much that it would be impossible for anyone to effectively to keep track of all of them. Actual alarm conditions that should require acknowledgement and response could easily get lost in the clutter on the screen.

A more effective means for event messaging is to have all messages logged in the system journal and have only alarm or other critical messages report to the monitoring station. These types of messages would include, but are not necessarily be limited to:

- Door forced and held alarms

- Access denied card reads

- Systems communication failures

- Supervision errors

- Door unlocks, including scheduled and manual actions

With most applications, messages can also be color coded based on priority. Red text could be used for door forced and door held alarms and multiple access denied card reads a card reader. Orange text could be used for supervision errors and blue text for manual actions. Programming event messaging in this manner will ensure all system events are recorded while at the same time limiting alarm monitoring station events to only those events critical to the safety and security of the facility.

Manual Actions

Manual actions are those actions that a system user performs from the system monitoring station. These are primarily remote door unlocking and locking, area lockdown events and shunting alarm. Whenever a user profile allows a system user to perform manual actions, the user should be required to enter a reason for the action in the comments section of the manual action window; including any required approvals received for the action. Another consideration would be to limit the types of manual actions a user may perform. A security officer in the security operations center may have privileges that allow them to unlock and lock "controlled\limited area" doors, while only supervisory level personnel have privileges to unlock and lock restricted area doors.

ACS System Integration

For the purposes of this section, integration refers to the integration of the access control and video management systems. As most ACS and VMS platforms are compatible, integration is usually accomplished through a graphical user interface (GUI) and does not require any significant programming other than linking the

VMS servers and cameras to the ACS and programming camera actions that associate alarm events with cameras. When properly integrated and programmed, a camera icon will pop up in an alarm message. When the system user clicks on the icon the camera associated with the door or area comes up on the monitoring screen for real-time viewing. This significantly cuts down on the time a user may otherwise have to spend finding the right camera in the VMS and then bringing it up to investigate the alarm.

Video Management System

As the bandwidth requirements for continuous live video monitoring and security industry standard video retention rates of 30-60 days can be very taxing on a company's IT infrastructure and support capabilities, an effective means for reducing both bandwidth and storage requirements is to only record on motion and limit live camera views to only a few critical security doors, reducing frames per second (fps) recoding to 12-16 fps and bringing up other live camera feeds for alarm and incident response\follow up.

When a CCTV camera is set to record on motion it continues to view an area 24 x 7. Whenever motion (a change is pixilation) is detected in a predefined area, the VMS application activates the record feature for the selected camera and video footage of the event is recorded. When setting a camera to record on motion, you have the option to set the video recording for a predefined time prior before and after motion was detected. This lets the user see what happened just before motion was detected as well as after motion stopped. In the event of an unauthorized entry, there will be a recording of the perpetrator's approach, break and\or enter and their direction of travel after they exited the area. In order to accomplish this VMS applications continually record on a loop and overwrite video footage every few minutes.

Assume that the image in Figure 12 is your loading dock and you just want to record video for the loading dock overhead door and personnel door and nothing else. In the motion detection window for the camera, set a grid for the area to you want recorded and then set the before and after time parameters. Say, 30 seconds before and 1 minute after motion detection. Any motion within the grid will automatically trigger video recording. If the overhead door or personnel door begin to open, recording will be triggered. If someone approaches the overhead door or personnel door, recording will also be triggered. This is a very effective method for recording only relevant video images without using up excessive amounts of storage space on the video server(s).

Figure 12: Motion Detection Grid

Care should be taken when programming pan-tilt-zoom (PTZ) cameras to ensure cameras cannot pan to view private property or into the windows of non-company buildings. This can be accomplished by presetting camera fields of view in the VMS application. Much like programming for record on motion, limits on the field of view can be set to restrict system user ability to pan the camera outside of predefined fields.

The video analytics capabilities of newer generation VMS systems are much more robust than older systems, making alarm monitoring and video association with alarm events and suspicious activities much more effective than the older standalone systems that may or may not be integrated with a facility's ACS.

As the internet is replete with both video footage and captured images from company VMS systems, organizations need implement protocols to reduce the likelihood of images from their systems being posted on line. This can be accomplished through a combination of written guidelines and setting system user privileges. Guidelines should spell out in detail who can request video images, the approval process for exporting and sharing images and the position title of the person who can export the images. The policy can state that video footage and images may not be provided anyone, including law enforcement, without prior approval of a designated company manager; and that only supervisory or management level personnel shall have system user privileges that allow them to export video images. This will go a long way in ensuring that system images are not shared and lessen the likelihood of adverse legal action as a result of images being shared publically.

Maintenance and Service

As with any building management system, EPSS require regularly scheduled preventative maintenance checks and services (PMCS) to maintain system functionality. Below are minimum suggested checks.

Daily Checks

- Supervision errors.

- Communication errors.

- Camera views of all cameras.

- PTZ camera functionality.

- Document and submit work request for all deviances noted.

Monthly \ Quarterly Checks

- Check door forced and held alarms at each door by physically causing alarms at the door(s).

- Check all door release buttons and electric crash bars for functionality.

- Check local audible alarms.

- Document and submit work request for all deviances noted.

Annual Checks and Services

- Perform all monthly\quarterly checks listed above.

- Clean and adjust devices; replace defective devices, as necessary.

- Check CCTV camera views, focus and clarity. Clean housings and lenses and refocus cameras, as necessary.

- Ensure application software and firmware is up to date. Download updates, as necessary.

Systems Monitoring

When people think of a security command center they often envision a large room with numerous flat screen CCTV monitors on the walls and a large console with multiple computer workstations where 2 – 5 security personnel continuously monitor CCTV cameras and security alarms. Although this was the predominant model in the past and is still in use by many organizations, it is outdated, overly expensive to equip and operate, and system users cannot monitor all cameras and systems with any degree of effectiveness.

"Based on the theory of attention economics, most security control centers and corresponding video surveillance systems today present security personnel with a wealth of information, leading to a poverty of attention. The aforementioned study (Green, 1999) showed a disturbing trend in operator performance:'

- Security operator performance degrades considerably after 20 minutes.'

- Security operators cannot effectively monitor multiple surveillance cameras and sensors.'

- Poor image quality accelerates this rate of degradation.'

- Viewing twice the number of cameras accelerates degradation by a factor of two."[11]

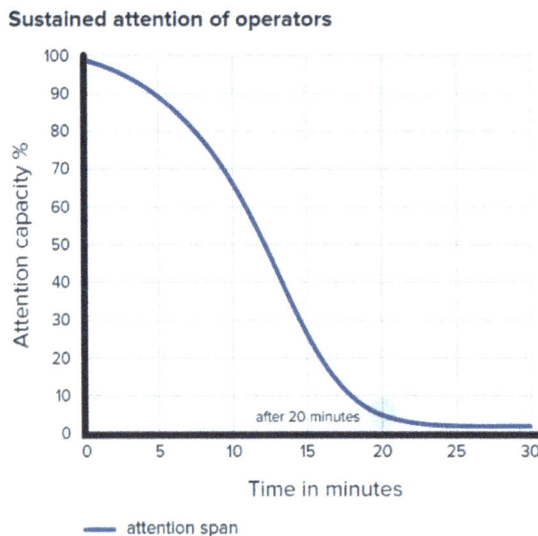

Figure 13: CCTV Camera Monitoring Span of Attention (Green, 1999)

In his 1971 article, "Designing Organizations for an Information-Rich World", Herbert Simon stated, "A wealth of information creates a poverty of attention."[12] Simon went on to opine that most technology systems are focused on providing as much information as possible without taking the human attention span into consideration. Consequently, these systems provide a surplus of information to people, when what was really needed are systems that filter out irrelevant information and highlight only items of interest (Simon 1996). The outcomes of both Green's and Simon's studies indicate that the traditional SOC model is not compatible with how the human brain works and processes information.

With today's security systems technology, most SOC's can now be run out of a cubicle in a small room; requiring nothing more than 2 – 3 desktop computers, a 3 – 5 monitor array, 1 mouse and 1 keyboard. Wall mounted flat screen monitors may also be also installed for event monitoring. An example might be one monitor to bring up CCTV cameras for event specific viewing and another monitor that is connected to a business news\weather cable TV package for monitoring important news and weather events. Depending on a company's national\global footprint and the SOC's role in emergency response and business resiliency plans, larger companies may require more than one workstation and up to 2 – 3 monitoring personnel.

Regardless of an organization's size, leveraging technology and properly programming and integrating systems can significantly reduce security operating costs while at the same time providing effective protective measures to meet the business's risk mitigation goals and strategies.

Moving Beyond Paper-Based Systems

Security – and especially contract security service providers – inherently relies on legacy paper-based systems for visitor management, lost and found property control, daily post activity logs, package delivery logs, incident reports, key control and other daily activities. Although these work well for recoding information, they are ineffective in that they are susceptible to human error and are very time consuming to review when searching for incident information or compiling data for security metrics and facility design planning.

Not everyone has good penmanship, spelling errors, mis-categorization of activity and incidents are not uncommon and the process is usually time-consuming on both the security officer and the security customer. When searching for incident reports, managers have to search through documents to find initial information, such as incident date, type and report number, then locate the report which may be in an office file or archived in boxes in a storage room. When trying to analyze personnel or vehicle traffic patterns for security metrics or a lobby or loading dock upgrade project, someone has to read all the logs, manually compile the information, enter it into a spreadsheet, insert charts and then turn it into a presentation for business unit managers and decision makers. This is can be a very time consuming process; and time is money. When human error is factored into the equation, the results of your efforts and resources expended might end up being a nothing more than a best guess. Lastly, paper-based systems are not an environmentally friendly process. A much more efficient and environmentally sustainable process would be to put as much of this information as possible in a database.

There are many visitor management, vehicle tracking and security incident report, activity log and risk management software applications on the market that can meet the needs of any business or facility model. Depending on the number of system user licenses\seats required, many of these applications can be costly to set up $25,000+, with annual licensing fees easily reaching or exceeding $10,000 - $20,000+. Most ACS manufactures offer a visitor management system that is compatible with their application, which is a viable approach for systems with an open architecture platform. Another approach to consider is leveraging existing business database applications for logging and storing information. A package tacking software already used by shipping & receiving could be used by security for logging deliveries at lobby desks and for lost and found property logging. *Remedy®, SAP® and Archibus®* are just three of many ticketing systems that are suitable and adaptable to meet physical security reporting needs. Since these systems are already in place and integrated across the organization, the only work required would be to identify basic information, field requirements and reporting parameters. Incident report fields could include category (Facilities, Safety, Security, etc.) and incident type.

- Facilities: HVAC, power outage, equipment malfunction, etc.

- Safety: Medical emergency, safety hazard, hazmat sill\leak, etc.

- Security: Theft, threat, suspicious person\activity, workplace violence, etc.

Some may argue that non-security personnel such as IT support staff may have access to the information. But this would also be the same case if a separate software package was purchased and installed on company servers. Information security can be easily accomplished through user privileges. Restricting non-security personnel access that limits administrative rights to application and server support functions but does not allow the SysAdmin to view user text entries will help to reduce the likelihood of sensitive security information being compromised.

Chapter 6

Key Management Program

One of the most basic forms of physical security is lock and key control. Yet, it is also one of the most misunderstood and mismanaged security programs in many organizations. The most common issues with mismanagement are inadequate or insufficient key hierarchy design, inferior lock and key systems, and lock and key control not properly managed and enforced.

Key Hierarchy

The key hierarchy is a masterplan\map of the lock and key structure for a company or facility. It can be for one facility or multiple facilities. The hierarchy sets the company standards on how locks are to be pinned and what types of keys can open a single lock or group of locks. It should list all master and sub-master keys\keyways and identify what types of doors\locks fall under each subset. When developing a key hierarchy, it is important to limit the number of levels in the hierarchy. Locksmiths recommend that a key hierarchy have no more than 4 – 5 levels. The reason for this is: the more levels there are in the hierarchy, the more cuts will be required in keys as you move down from the master keys to individual lock keys. The more cuts in the key, the weaker the key can become, in turn resulting in keys that could easily breakoff in a lock.

The first step in developing a key hierarchy is to segregate different business functions, such as Facilities, IT, Safety, etc. and then identify subgroups for each function. For Facilities, you have electrical rooms, mechanical rooms, offices, storage rooms, etc. With this structure, your Facilities key hierarchy would look something like this:

- Site Grand Master (GM): Opens all doors

- Facilities Master (FM): Opens all Facilities doors\locks and perimeter doors

- Electrical Master (EM): Opens all electrical rooms

  - Individual electrical rooms keyed to this master

- Mechanical Master (MM): Opens all HVAC\mechanical rooms

  - Individual mechanical rooms keyed to this master

- Office Master (OM): Opens all offices and office storage rooms

  - All offices and general storage rooms are keyed to this master

- Housekeeping Master (HM): Opens all janitorial closets and cleaning supply storage rooms.

Below is a sample key hierarchy for a hypothetical multisite pharmaceutical company where there is a Great Grand Master (GGM) key that would open all doors for multiple buildings\sites, and a site GM key that would open all doors for a specific site.

Under the hierarchy depicted in Figure 14, an electrical contractor working on site could be issued an EM key for access to all electrical rooms, or individual electrical room keys as opposed to an FM or GM key. Similarly, a telecomm contractor working on site could be issued an IDF master (IDM) key for all IDF rooms, or individual IDF room keys.

When the master key system is structured properly and sub-master keys are issued, the number of locks\rooms that may need to be rekeyed if a key is lost are limited to just those locks that fall under the sub-master. Whereas, if a GM key is issued and is then subsequently lost, the entire facility may need to be rekeyed.

```
                        ┌──────────────┐
                        │   GREAT      │
                        │   GRAND      │
                        │   MASTER     │
                        └──────┬───────┘
                        ┌──────┴───────┐
                        │   SITE       │
                        │   GRAND      │
                        │   MASTER     │
                        └──────┬───────┘
```

FACILITIES MASTER	SAFETY MASTER	IT MASTER	LAB MASTER	REGULATORY MASTER
ELECTRICAL MASTER	HAZMAT STORAGE MASTER	DATA CENTER MASTER	VIVARIUM MASTER	LEGAL FILE STORAGE MASTER
MECHANICAL MASTER	FIRST AID STATION MASTER	IDF MASTER	BL-1\2 MASTER	REGULATORY FILE STORAGE MASTER
OFFICE MASTER		MDF MASTER	BL-2+ MASTER	
JANITORIAL MASTER			QUALITY CONTROL LAB	

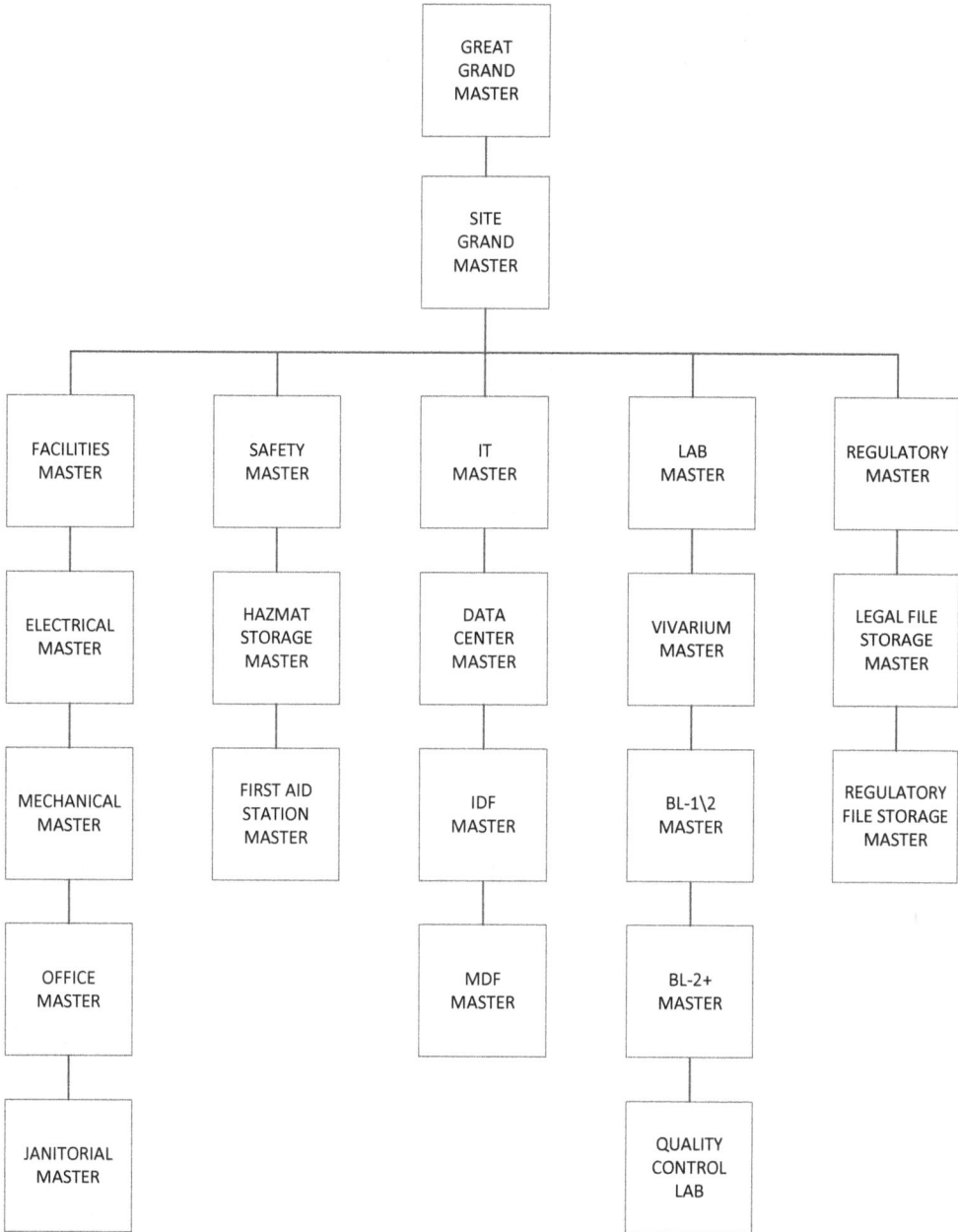

Figure 14: Sample Multiple Site Key Hierarchy

Lock and Key Management

The only way to achieve effective lock and key management is to have comprehensive guidelines in place that are strictly enforced. Regardless of the electronic access control systems installed or the type of locks and keys used, if the key management program and key control procedures are not adhered to, facility security will remain in constant jeopardy of being compromised. There are numerous instances where keys were not collected from a person whose employment was terminated and that person returned and stole property or caused damaged to company property or equipment.

Lock and Key Types

Standard -v- Interchangeable Core Locks

Companies should always use commercial grade locks and keys. There are two basic types of locks and locksets: standard lock and interchangeable core. The standard lock is a self-contained locking system where the mechanical workings of the lock are contained within the lock and usually require changing out the lock or lockset or calling in a locksmith to rekey the lock if rekeying is required. Due to the amount of labor required to rekey these types of locks, service calls could be expensive, with rekeying an entire facility costing $125,000 or more.

While the initial outlay for an interchangeable core (IC) system is slightly more expensive than a standard lock system, it is actually less expensive and more secure in the long run. The mechanical workings of the lock are contained in a core that can be installed in or removed from the lock (cylindrical lockset, mortise lockset, padlock, etc.) using a *control key*. After 5 minutes of training any facility technician or security officer can swap out an IC. The actual process of changing out an IC takes less than 1 minute. Most companies that use IC locks usually keep a stock of cores on site for use when a key is lost or stolen, or when keying construction locks. The cost of rekeying a facility with an IC system can be as much as 50% - 75% less expensive than it would be for a standard lock system.

Lock Security Levels

There are three common types of commercial locks: commercial, restricted keyway and high security locks. All three are adaptable to the standard and IC lock systems. The big difference between these locks lays primarily in how the locks are pinned, the ability to obtain key blanks and have keys cut, and the lock's resistance to surreptitious manipulation (lock picking).

Standard Commercial Locks

Standard commercial locks work well for most business environments, including office buildings, manufacturing facilities, educational institutions and most research and development facilities. Commercial locks come in 6, 7 and 8 pin configurations. The more pins (tumblers) in a lock, the more secure it will be and the more difficult it will be to pick.

Restricted Keyways

A restricted keyway lock is a commercial lock where the keyway design is restricted on a 2 – 5 state regional basis, with no 2 companies within a region being able to own the same keyway. A company purchases the keyway from a locksmith who is the sole provider of the keyway for the company and is the only person who can purchase key blanks from the manufacturer and cut keys. Additionally, the lock owner must designate and provide signatures of a limited number of people (2 – 3) who can order keys\locks\cores from the locksmith. This is an effective means of ensuring that keys for a facility cannot be purchased and cut at a hardware store or by a random locksmith.

High Security Locks

High security locks are restricted keyways with added lock and key features that make a lock extremely difficult to pick. These include added features in the lock and channels on the key that allow only a specific key to fit into a lock. Medeco, which has been the industry leader in high security locks and provides locks for banks and high security government facilities, uses a patented technology where a tumbler not only must rise into position, but must also twist as it rises to fit into the tumbler channel.

Most commercial lock manufacturers offer restricted keyway and high security locks with compatible keyway design features that allow companies to blend restricted keyway and high security locks in their key hierarchy design. If a company wants to use high security locks on certain doors (hazmat storage rooms, data center, R&D labs, etc.) and only restricted keyways for other locks, the keyway and bitting scheme can be designed in such a way where high security locks have one keyway design and all other locks have another design feature, allowing only high security keys to be inserted into high security locks. From a master key perspective, keyways can be designed to allow a master key to open both types of locks. As high security locks are more expensive than other locks, this is a good way to increase lock security without breaking the bank in the process.

Lock and Key Control

The linchpin of any key management program is how locks and keys are controlled. This includes the storage, issue and return of locks and keys. Following are minimum high level lock and key control guidelines that should be included in any key management program.

- A primary and alternate key control program manager should be appointed. The key control program manager has overall responsibility for management and administration of the company\facility key management program.

- All locks and keyways should be pinned in accordance with the company key hierarchy. Note: Key hierarchy and bitting lists should not be included in the facility security standards or key control procedures documents. These are sensitive security documents that should be treated as confidential proprietary information.

- Only company padlocks or cable locks should be used to secure company areas or equipment; such as doors, fence gates and grounds keeping equipment.

- All keys should be clearly marked with "Do Not Duplicate".

- Key identification numbering should be such that the marking does not indicate what the key is for. Marks such as GGM, GM, FM, etc. are strongly discouraged.

- Keys, key blanks and lock cores should be stored in a locked cabinet or container, in a secured area.

- Key rings issued for temporary use should be of a tamper resistant design so that keys cannot be removed from the ring prior to return.

- A key should be issued only to individuals who have a legitimate and official requirement for the key.
  - A requirement for access alone, when access can be accomplished by other means (such as unlocking doors, request for entry, intercoms, card readers, etc.), shall not convey automatic entitlement to a key.
  - Only the lowest level key(s) in a key hierarchy should be issued when keys are issued for temporary use.

- No person should be issued a GGM or GM key. GGM and GM keys may be placed in a firefighter Knox box for emergency access purposes.

- All keys must be signed for upon receipt and signed in when they are returned.

  - The use of electronic key cabinets where a cardholder's badge or PIN code can be programmed for specific key access is a viable means for enhanced key control. Electronic key cabinets can be integrated with most access control systems. When a person's badge access is suspended or terminated their access to the key cabinet will no longer work.

- All keys remain the property of the company and must be returned when the reason for which they were issued is no longer valid. Managers or Human Resources representatives should be responsible for collecting keys from terminated employees and returning the key(s) to security or the key control manager.

- Key-holders are responsible for the security of the keys they are issued and should not duplicate any key or lend their key(s) to any other person.

- Lost, stolen or missing keys must be immediately reported to security or the key control manager.

- Keys, key blanks and cores should be inventoried on a regular basis to ensure they are accounted for.

  - Temporary use keys should be inventoried daily.

  - All keys, key blanks and cores should be inventoried on at least a quarterly basis.

- Guidelines for re-coring\keying locks whenever a key is lost or stolen should be outlined in key management program guidelines.

  - Loss of a room key should require that the lock be changed out.

  - Loss of a master key should require the change out of all locks under that master key hierarchy.

Chapter 7

Selecting a Security Provider

In most markets there will be a number of good contract security providers from which a company can choose to provide security services for their facility. When evaluating security providers to determine if they are capable of meeting the company's security needs, the service provider should be evaluated not only on their ability to provide cost effective services, but how much industry related experience they have, their management support, ability to meet event and emergency staffing needs, and value added services. Most regional, national and international security service providers will have the experience and support mechanisms in place to meet the needs of almost every facility. However, they also provide boilerplate or cookie cutter programs that may need to be modified to meet the specific needs of a facility's business model.

Identifying Security Staffing Needs

Just as there is such a thing as not enough security, there is also such a thing as too much security. Not having enough security increases the risk of property theft and vandalism and decreases the ability to effectively respond to incidents and potential life threatening emergencies. On the other hand, too much security can actually hinder the business process, unduly inconvenience employees, contractors and visitors, and take a good chunk out of the security budget. The object is to find a happy medium that is both cost effective and reasonable.

Whether looking for security services for a new facility or considering a new provider, the first step is to determine what the facility security needs are, what the minimum qualifications for security personnel assigned to the facility should be and what your expectations of the service provider's management team are. This develops a baseline from which further planning and a request for proposal (RFP) can be developed. As actual staffing levels and needs can vary significantly from one business model to another, as well as from one site to another within a company, the goal of this section is to provide high level guidelines that can be modified to meet the specific needs of a facility's business model.

There are nine key factors that come into play when determining guard force structure and service provider capabilities: Business Model, Facility\Campus Size, Location, Hours of Operation, Security Systems, Emergency Response Requirements and Company Events.

Business Model

The first thing to consider is the facility's business model and any regulatory requirements on the business. A regulated environment will inherently have much stricter physical security controls than a nonregulated environment and require a stronger security presence and more industry specific training. While a corporate or multitenant office building may require a receptionist during business hours and a patrol officer during nonbusiness hours, a manufacturing facility will most likely have multiple shifts and multiple building access points for employees and visitors, and loading docks where materials and product are shipped and received; requiring more security personnel to provide adequate security protection for the facility.

Facility\Campus Size

For large facilities and campuses with multiple buildings, the amount of square footage of all facilities on the campus becomes an important factor in determining staffing levels, especially when security officers are required to perform facility\campus foot patrols and tours. On average, security officers will walk a total 8 – 12 miles in an 8-hour shift conducting 4 patrols of a 500,000 square multistory building; with each tour of the building taking approximately 1 hour.

The easiest way to determine how tours should be designed and conducted and the amount of time required to do a tour (Tt) is by calculating the distance (D) in feet required to walk the tour route, divide the total distance by 5,280 (feet in 1 mile) (M), and then multiply the result by the average human walking speed (WS) of 3 miles per hour; or 20 minutes per mile.

In the following example, the total distance to complete one tour is 10,000 feet. Based on an average human walking speed of 20 minutes per mile, it will take the security officer 38 minutes to walk the tour route.

$$\frac{D}{M} \; x \; WS = Tt$$

$$\frac{10,000}{5,280} = 1.89$$

$$1.89 \; x \; 20 = 37.9 \, minutes$$

The actual time required to conduct the tour will increase based on the type of tour, number of floors and facilities, number of tour points and building infrastructure and support equipment that must be checked during the tour. When these factors and security officer breaks are taken into consideration, a reasonable time allotment would be 1 hour for this tour; allowing for a 15 minute security officer break and time to complete shift paperwork and submit any work requests for discrepancies noted during the tour.

Another consideration when it comes to facility\campus size is the number of security officers on duty during any given shift. Like regular employees, security officers need to be allotted lunch and personal breaks during their shifts. While roving security officers can easily take breaks during their shifts, security officers at stationary posts will need to be relieved for their breaks. Many organizations consider bringing in a relief officer who can provide breaks to officers at stationary posts. The relief officer can be a part-time security employee who comes in a few hours after a shift starts, works a 4 – 5 hour shift giving breaks and then leaves for the day. If the shift runs 7:00am – 3:00pm, a good shift for the relief officer might be 9:00am – 1:00pm\2:00pm. The best break officer to security officer ratio is 1 break officer for every 4 – 5 stationary security officers on duty. This ratio is based on each stationary officer receiving two 15 minute personal breaks and one 30 minute lunch break during their assigned shift; or 1 hour per stationary security officer per shift. It is also important to factor in the time it takes the break officer to go from one post to the other.

Location

Facilities located in high crime areas will require a stronger security presence than facilities in rural and low crime areas. If the facility is located in a high crime area, if there is a large indigenous transient population or there are a number of registered level 3 sex offenders within 2 miles of the facility, security officers should be available to provide after-hours onsite escorts (i.e., building to building, to\from parking lots, etc.) for personnel working late in the facility. The facility may also require more exterior patrols of the property than if it were located in an area with a lower risk profile.

Hours of Operation

If there are multiple shift changes, then coverage for personnel entrances should be planned so as not to coincide with standard facility shift change times. If security is changing shifts at the same time as other personnel working at the facility, security officers could easily miss something as simple as someone without a badge as they might be detracted by their shift change routine. For the same reasons, if the facility does not have shift workers and operates on a 9:00am – 5:00pm or similar schedule, lobby and other personnel entrance shifts should start at least 1/2 hour prior to opening time and last until at least 1/2 hour after normal closing time.

Security Systems

A well-integrated physical security program blends technology and security staffing to achieve optimal facility protection. While a technology only scenario may work well for a small facility with minimal non-employee visitors, manufacturing, R&D, distribution centers, data centers and similar facilities will usually require a blended solution with a 24-hour security presence. Whenever onsite security is responsible for monitoring site security and building systems, the security officers hired for these positions need to have above average computer skills, be able to multitask and have the ability react quickly and effectively in stressful situations. Understanding the systems the security officer is required to monitor and their responsibilities in alarm and incident response will help to identify the caliber of security officer required for the position.

Emergency Response Duties

Security is an integral part of a facility's emergency response plans. In many situations security provides initial response to emergency incidents. They are often called on to perform emergency First Aid\CPR\AED in medical and injury related incidents. If security officers are required to perform these duties, they need to trained and certified to perform them.

Company Event & Incident Staffing

Another point for consideration is the frequency of company events and emergency\short notice staffing needs. If the company has seasonal events, large company meetings or other such events, the security provider should be able to provide additional personnel for these events. The contractor should also be able to staff emergency or short notice staffing needs, such as additional patrols for pending strikes or demonstrations, a threat against the company, workforce restructure activities and business resiliency plan needs.

Evaluating Security Providers

There are two types of contract models to choose from when evaluating a security service provider's ability to meet a company's needs: *Single Source and Blended*.

- *Single Source:* Security services are provided by a sole contract security provider. The contractor provides all personnel and security operations support on a local, regional, national or global scale.

- *Blended:* A blended service model is one where a national or international contractor security provider subcontracts to another contractor to provide personnel and security operations support in a region where they do not have a physical presence. The company signs only one contract with the selected provider for all security service operations and the contractor assigns a regional\national\global account manager and single point of contact for management oversight of all contracted and subcontracted security staffing, operations support and billing.

Regardless of the contract security services model used, the security contractor and their subcontractor's need to be able to provide the types of services required to meet a facility's protection needs. Such things as training programs (basic and advanced security officer training and industry specific training), uniforms and equipment, scheduling practices, payroll and billing practices, and industry specific experience will help when weeding through contractors and finding the security provider who can best meet the facility's business needs. The more qualified and experienced the company, the better the quality of service will be and the less work the facility's security program manager will have to do in day-to-day security operation management.

Company Size

Does the security contractor have enough employees to meet facility staffing needs? Although most security providers can provide a few hundred hours or less of security coverage per week, many small local companies may have difficulty consistently providing 800 or more hours of coverage a week. In addition to standard weekly coverage, the security provider should be able to provide recurring coverage for company events and emergency or last minute coverage for protests, demonstrations, labor disputes or other such events that the facility may be subject to from time to time. When considering emergency staffing capabilities, it is important the determine the security provider's ability staff posts in the event of a major weather event or other disaster that may affect an entire city or region. If there is a blizzard that significantly inhibits transportation or shuts down roadways, what are the contractor's procedures for shift scheduling and providing food to security officers who may be stuck at the facility until roadways are cleared? If it is a major disaster or event where access to an area is restricted to authorized personnel only, what method does the contractor have in place that will allow security officers to pass through road blocks or checkpoints to get to the facility?

Experience and Turnover

Every industry is different and each comes with its own idiosyncrasies and related risks. A manufacturing facility comes with large amounts of material movement, hazardous machinery and the potential for labor disputes if there is a unionized workforce. A pharmaceutical R&D facility usually has large amounts of hazardous materials and is highly regulated. The company could also be the target of animal rights activist and\or extremist activities. A distribution center could have large amounts of highly pilferable finished product. When screening potential security providers, ask them how much experience they have in the company's industry. Ask them to explain what they believe are the most significant risks related to the business and facility. Ask the provider for a minimum of three industry related references and call those references. If the security program manager is part of a local industry chapter (International Facility Management Association, American Biological Safety Association, American Society for Industry Security, etc.), contact other members and ask them for a reference. It is also a good idea to check the Better Business Bureau for any complaints against the company. Although online sites like Glass Door, Rip Off Report and Indeed may contain employee feedback on the contractor, most of the people who post in these forums are previous employees and the information they provide is usually not verified or verifiable.

Annual employee turnover rates in the contract security industry historically run between 50% - 150%. These high turnover rates can be attributed to the low pay rates and limited employee benefits programs common throughout the industry. Turnover rates also provide a good indication of employee training and job satisfaction. Employees who are trained and compensated with fair wages and employee benefits experience greater job satisfaction and will remain with the company for a longer period of time. The security provider's turnover rates will also give you a good idea of the potential experience level of their security officers. High turnover rates mean a greater potential of having security officers with limited security and industry experience. A 25% turnover over rate means there is a good chance that 25% of the security staff will not have significant security experience.

Employment & Assignment Prescreening

The contractor's standard pre-employment screening should include, as a minimum:

- Verification of authorization to work in the U.S. or applicable country.

- Verification of social security (social insurance) number through E-Verify or other applicable verification process.

- 5 years employment history verification. More may be required based on regulatory, state licensing or industry requirements inherent to the site.

- Pre-employment drug screening for drugs of abuse (where applicable law permits).

- 7 year criminal records check (where applicable law permits).

- Sex offender registry check (where applicable law permits).

- Education verification. Security officers should have at least a high school diploma or equivalent (GED). Verification should include check of school records and college transcripts.

In addition to pre-employment screening, managers may consider pre-assignment screening. This is especially useful when working in a regulated environment, when hiring for a supervisor\management level position or the position requires technical skills such as security operations center duties.

- Possession of security guard or officer license where required by law.

- Completion of any state required security guard training requirements.

- Motor vehicle driver's record check if security is required to operate a company owned or leased vehicle.

- Citizenship verification if required by regulatory guidelines.

- Preferably, security officers should have at least 1 year security industry experience. However, this is sometimes difficult to achieve with the high turnover rate inherent to the contract security service industry.

- Supervisors should have 2 – 5 years security industry experience, or at least 1 year security experience and 1 year of supervisory experience.

- Site security managers or supervisors responsible for overall onsite security services at the facility should have minimum 3 – 5 years security management experience, or a minimum 2 year college degree and 3 years security experience.

- If security officers will be armed, possession of a current firearms permit and successful completion of a firearms safety and qualification course.

- Complex or regulated environments may dictate that security officers, supervisors and managers have direct industry related security experience prior to assignment.

Security Officer Pay & Benefits

Historically, contract security officer pay rates are low and benefits, if offered, are usually minimal or overly expensive for the officer. A review of 2017 U.S. average annual salaries showed that security officers are compensated on par with cleaners and landscaping laborers.

Job Title	Annual Salary	Hourly Wage
Security Officer	$25,280	$12.15
Cleaner	$24,190	$11.63
Groundskeeper	$25,438	$12.23

U.S. Census Bureau – 2017 U.S. Average Pay Rates. Local rates may vary.

The reason the prevailing security officer wage rate is on par with cleaners and grounds keepers is because the security officer job is classified as unskilled labor in HR and government labor categories. People working in this category are defined as: *An unskilled worker is an employee who does not use reasoning or intellectual abilities in their line of work. These workers are typically found in positions that involve manual labor such as packager, assembler, or apprentice, or farm worker. (www.mightyrecruiter.com).* When you consider the duties and responsibilities of a security officer in business environments, they are far from being unskilled employees. In addition to controlling building access, security officers monitor and respond to building and security system alarms, analyze video footage to investigate incidents, respond to and provide medical assistance in medical emergencies, coordinate emergency response to a multitude of other site emergency conditions, interview victims and witnesses of incidents, write incidents reports that may be used in civil or criminal cases, use various computer software applications in the daily performance of their assigned duties and must be able to respond calmly and effectively in stressful situations.

The minimum employee standards for a security officer are also more stringent than unskilled labor jobs. While there are usually no minimum education or experience requirements for cleaners and groundkeepers, security officers must meet minimum education requirements, pass drug screening and criminal background checks, be fluent in the predominant spoken and written language of the country they are in, may need to be multilingual, must be computer literate and able to learn and use a multitude of business and security applications, and complete job specific training, including any state legally mandated security officer training and certification requirements. In order to attract and retain skilled employees in a security industry that is becoming more and more reliant on technology based approaches, security officer wages must rise to meet the skilled labor requirements of the job; *a job that requires workers to have specialized training or a learned skill-set to perform the work.* As the old adage goes, you get what you pay for. If you pay for unskilled labor, you will get unskilled labor. If you pay $2.00 - $2.50 more an hour than the area's prevailing security officer wage rate, you will attract and retain more qualified security officers.

Benefits are also a key factor in attracting and retaining motivated and qualified employees in any industry. Employees who are offered vacation and personal days and good medical benefits at a reasonable cost are more likely to be satisfied in the job and will remain with that job longer than those with minimal, costly or no benefits at all. In order to keep costs and bill rates low and remain competitive within the contract security industry, many contractors offer minimal employee benefits. Such as 1 week vacation and baseline medical benefits that can prove to be very expensive or even cost prohibitive based on the employee's wage rate. It is not that uncommon where medical and dental benefits consume 25% - 45% of a security officer's weekly paycheck.

In summary, the question decision makers need to ask is… What is the safety and security of my company and workforce really worth? Offering above average area pay and benefits will ensure a more qualified and motivated security force is hired and retained, leading to a more safe and secure workplace.

Training

The types and quality of training programs the security provider offers its employees will have a significant impact on quality of the service. The security provider should have a pre-assignment basic security officer training program that teaches basic security skills to new employees, and an on-the-job training (OJT) program that provides security officers and supervisors with the knowledge and job specific skills required to perform their assigned duties at the facility. At no time should a security officer be scheduled or allowed to work a permanent post at the facility unless they have successfully completed the site's OJT program. This may be waived in certain situations where a security officer is on site for a special event or detail however, the officer should never be allowed to work any other post without proper site-specific training.

Pre-assignment minimum training requirements should include:

- A minimum of 4 (preferably 8 - 16) hours of training dedicated to general security roles and responsibilities. Although many contract security providers say they provide 4 hours of new hire orientation training, it is not uncommon that 1 hour or more of that time is dedicated to drug screening, issuing uniforms, completion of income tax withholding documents, company employment and benefits documents, and review of the provider's equal opportunity employment, anti-harassment, alcohol and drug abuse, workplace violence, disciplinary action and other corporate policies.

- Successful completion of AED\CPR\First Aid training if the company requires security officers to be certified in AED\CPR\First Aid. If a security officer is assigned to the site and they do not possess the required certification and respond to a medical emergency that requires them to perform AED\CPR\First Aid, they may not be able to perform the emergency lifesaving tasks required of their position. This could place the wellbeing of the victim in jeopardy. In the event that the security officer's inability to perform basic lifesaving measures contributes to further injury or death, the business could also be subject to negligent liability claims.

- Completion of any regulatory or state mandated security officer licensing or training requirements.

- Review and signing of the company nondisclosure agreement for facility the security officer, supervisor or manager will be assigned to.

On-the-Job Training requirements are more subjective and wholly dependent on the business environment, regulatory guidelines, position assignment and complexity of the position. A security officer working in a security operations center will require more technical training than a security officer working at an employee entrance or lobby post. Hence the OJT program for each should be different, with the officer working the security operations center receiving more training in both content and time. Following is a framework for minimum OJT training requirements.

- Security Officer and Receptionist: 16 to 40 hours of job specific training. Access control; visitor management; phone etiquette; patrol duties; vehicle operations, maintenance and service; incident response; review of security policy and procedure documents.

- Security Operations Center Officer: Completion of security officer OJT and a minimum of 24 – 40 hours training in electronic security systems monitoring and emergency response and notification procedures.

- Security Supervisor: Completion of security officer and security operations center officer OJT and a minimum of 8 hours supervisor specific duties and responsibilities.

- Security Manager: Although the site manager\supervisor may not work at a security post, they need to have a good understanding of the security program and the duties performed by the security staff they manage. Assuming the manager has a strong physical security background, training should be 24 – 40 hours on general security officer duties and responsibilities and the guiding principles of the business' physical security program.

- All assigned contract security staff should complete all contractor and site specific safety, business code of conduct and regulatory training requirements within the required training windows.

- Monthly\quarterly drill training to maintain proficiency in emergency response procedures.

Scheduling Practices

How a security provider goes about making and filling schedules has a significant impact on security service quality and cost of services. The stubby pencil schedule is o.k. for smaller facilities, but schedules can become difficult to develop and confusing to follow when security coverage starts reaching 1,000 hours or more a week. A service provider with an automated scheduling system will usually have less difficulty in scheduling and filling security posts than one that doesn't.

If it is an especially large facility or campus that requires thousands of hours of coverage, the security provider will most likely have to draw employees from existing accounts to fill vacation and scheduled time off openings. This is can also be true when it comes to staffing company events. Whenever the security provider pulls from existing accounts to cover schedule openings, overtime can become a very difficult thing to track and control. Security officers could very well be leaving a shift at their primary facility, show up for a shift at another facility, then coming back to pull another shift at the first facility they worked at. Hence, the quality of the security officer performance will decrease. If the security provider will be drawing from outside accounts to fill the schedule, ask them what controls they have in place to prevent security officers from working triple shifts. Ideally, a security officer should not work more than 12 hours in a 24 hour period. However, 16 hour shifts are not uncommon in the contract security industry and seeing 16 hour shifts on a schedule shouldn't be of too much concern, as long as the security provider can show proof that they have a verifiable system in place to prevent excessive overtime scheduling and resulting security officer fatigue.

Payroll and Billing Practices

Security payrolls and invoices are based on payroll sign-in sheets that security officers sign when they report for work; and again when they leave work. There is usually a blank space on the sign-in sheet next to the person's shift for the security supervisor's initials. The payroll sign-in sheet will normally identify what security officer worked what post and at what times. The security provider also may use a combination of a payroll sign-in sheet and a post locator sheet. When there are a lot of security officers on duty at the same time and multiple post starting times, it is a lot easier to have everyone sign-in once and then post them as necessary throughout the facility. The sign-in sheets tell you who was on duty at what time. The post locator sheets tell you who worked what post and at what time. Either one or both of these documents are submitted to the company's payroll department for billing and invoicing.

A good practice is to ask the security provider to submit a copy of all post locator and payroll sign-in sheets for the facility. If the payroll sign-in sheets have security officer social security numbers on them, have the security provider provide a copy with the social security numbers blocked out. With these documents the security program manager will be able to identify which posts were or were not filled and how many hours an individual security officer has worked on any given day. They are also good for determining who was working at a particular post during a particular incident and are very good for settling any invoicing disputes over security coverage. If the security provider does not have some type of payroll sign-in and\or post locator system in place, or insists there is no way a copy of these documents can be provided, consideration should be given to finding another contractor for the facility.

Uniforms and Equipment

There are three basic styles of security uniforms. The business look (blazer, slacks, shirt & tie), the business casual look (shirt and dress slacks) and the police look. The uniform choice a manager makes should be based on the business environment and the image the company wants to project. The blue shirt and dark pants police-look works very well in manufacturing and distribution center environments, whereas the business look is more suited for the multitenant or corporate office building. The business casual look can also fit well in most industrial and office environments. There is also the option of having security officers in high visibility customer facing positions, such as main lobby posts, in the business look uniform and all other security personnel in the business casual uniform. Again, it is a matter of functionality and the image the company wants to project.

Another thing to look for is availability of radios and building tour equipment. In order for security to be effective and respond to both routine and emergency situations, security officers need to be able to communicate with each other. If the facility does not have radios, then the contractor should be able to provide radios for the site. As a minimum, all security supervisors and roving\break officers should have a radio. If security officers are required to perform building\property tours, the contractor should be able to provide an automated tour system for logging and keeping track of when tours were conducted and what tour stations where hit. If a security vehicle is required for large campus or multisite security patrols, the contractor should be able to provide a clearly marked security vehicle.

Supervision

How the security provider supervises its security officers and its supervisor to security officer ratio will greatly enhance or reduce the quality of service. Supervisors need industry specific experience and they need to be mobile. A security supervisor who is posted at a stationary post is nothing more than an access control\property control security officer with the additional duty of supervising employees they cannot visit at their workstations. Supervisors need to be able to check up on security officers posted throughout the facility, respond to any routine and emergency situations, and effectively supervise the security staff. The supervisor to security officer ratio is also a key to quality service. One security supervisor cannot directly supervise much more than 10 security officers and be expected to do so with a great deal of effectiveness or efficiency. In situations where the security staffing level is reduced to two security officers during nonbusiness hours, such as a patrol officer and lobby\operations center officer, consider making one officer the lead security officer and compensate that officer slightly more than the regular security officer wage. Doing so will ensure that there will always be someone on duty that is responsible and accountable for security operations on the shift.

Another supervision concern is the lone security officer who is posted at a facility during after-hours times. If there is only one security officer on duty, the security provider should have some type of after-hours call in procedures. The security officer should have a radio and\or access to a telephone and be required to call in to the contractor's security control center every hour during their shift. The security provider should also have a system in place for responding to the site in the event the security officer fails to call in at the designated times. This is not just to ensure a security officer is not sleeping on duty. There have been many instances where a lone security officer was seriously injured or suffered a major medical event and they were unable to make their scheduled call-in; with the security officer being found unconscious only after someone went to the site or when an employee came to work in the morning. A good security provider will have a mobile\roving supervisor on duty that checks up on static security posts and responds to incidents at them.

Cost of Services

Contract security providers offer two billing rates: *standard and premium.* The standard rate is the normal hourly billing rate for security services, with bill rates directly related to position and pay rates. Since the hourly pay rate for a security officer and supervisor are different, the hourly billing rate for each will also be different. If you have different rates for different positions, such as a security operations center officer, lobby receptionist and patrol officer, the hourly bill rate for each will vary accordingly. The same holds true for premium or overtime bill rates. The difference being that the premium rate is usually 1.5 times higher than the standard bill rate and is usually the rate charged for holidays worked and short notice (less than 72-hour notice) detail requests or detail hours that exceed more that 5% of the facility's standard weekly hours of coverage.

For general budget planning purposes, the standard markup across the contract security industry for guard services is 1.28 – 1.32. For a security officer making $12.50 per hour the average bill rate is $16.00 - $16.50 per hour of service. For supervisors making $18.00 per hour the average bill rate will be $23.04 - $23.76 per hour of service. This rate includes the contractor's costs to hire, train and uniform employees, insurance premiums, taxes, interest rates and other overhead expenses.

Instead of choosing an hourly bill rate for each position, businesses may choose a blended hourly rate that combines all pay\bill rates to come up with an average hourly rate for all services provided. It is hard to say which bill rate method will work best for any given organization. Facilities with fairly stable security coverage requirements and minimal detail coverage may find the individual hourly bill rate works best for them. Facilities in less stable environments and that experience numerous detail requests throughout the year may find a blended rate works best for them. It is also important to note that hourly bill rates should not include any leased vehicles or other equipment that may be required for the job. These charges should be listed as separate invoice line items or be charged separately on an equipment invoice.

A cost saving method worth considering is to have contractor employee benefits, such as medical, dental and vision care, billed separately as a pass-through and not include these costs in the standard hourly bill rate. Since the tax breaks for companies that provide medical coverage to a workforce are more favorable than the standard business deduction, even if the combined adjusted hourly service rate and pass-through medical expense would equate to the same 1.28 – 1.32 markup rate, the company can still save money on its taxes due to the favorable tax treatment of healthcare benefits provided.

Some contractors offer two types of payment options: *30-day payment and advance payment.* In most instances security services are billed in arrears for services provided and payment is due within 30-days of receipt of invoice. Some contractor security providers offer an advance payment option where a discount (usually ~5%) is deducted from the standard cost of services if the services are paid for in advance as opposed to billed in arrears. If the cost of service is paid for in advance, a credit can be issued for any services that were paid for in advance, but not provided during the invoice period.

Performance and Penalty Clauses

Performance and penalty clauses, which are common throughout the private contract security industry, are a way to keep the security provider in check and ensure quality security services. The performance clause outlines minimum acceptable performance standards and identifies unacceptable security standards. The performance clause can be invoked to justify not paying for unacceptable security services. Some of the most common items in a performance clause are sleeping on duty, unacceptable appearance and nonperformance of duty. If a security officer is found asleep on duty the customer should not have to pay for the time the security officer was at that post. The same holds true for security officers who show up in unkempt\dirty uniforms, or have very poor personal hygiene. Nor should a customer have to pay for security officers who do not enforce the facility's security policies and procedures. If they're not doing the job they were hired to do, then the customer shouldn't have to pay for the substandard services.

The penalty clause on the other hand accesses a penalty in the form of a credit or reduced billing rate for failure to provide services. The penalty clause is most commonly used when there are open posts. An open post is any scheduled security post that is not filled or is abandoned and left unstaffed without good cause (e.g., emergency situations). If the security provider fails to fill a scheduled security post (with the exception of last minute detail orders), or a security officer abandons a security post without proper relief, the penalty clause can be invoked to have the security provider pay for the time that the post was left unstaffed.

This is how the penalty clause works. The security provider is assessed a penalty for open posts because they increase the risks of unauthorized access to the facility, property theft and overall personal safety. It is also a form of reimbursement for expenses incurred to fill\staff the post with non-service provider personnel. When the security provider fails to fill a scheduled security post, the customer does not pay for coverage for the time the post was left open. In addition to not paying for the coverage, the security provider pays a penalty (unusually in the form of a billing credit) for each hour, or portion thereof, that the post was left open. This works out to a double credit that goes directly to the security budget bottom line.

Example:

Description	Hourly Bill Rate	Credit
8 hours open post	$22.00	($176.00)
8 hour penalty credit	$22.00	($176.00)
Total Invoice Credit:		($352.00)

Most security providers will not tell you about performance and penalty clauses. You will have to bring them up yourself and, if possible, have them added into the contract or attached as an addendum. The performance clause will be a relatively easy one to negotiate. The penalty clause will be a little more difficult to reach agreement on, but that should not preclude a manager from bringing it up during the contract negotiation.

Contractor Liability

In addition to requiring workers compensation, minimum liability and umbrella insurance policies, businesses should scrutinize the limits of liability clause in their security service contract. It is not uncommon for security service agreements to be worded in such a fashion as to not hold the security provider liable for nonperformance or negligence on the part of the company or its employees in the performance of the their duties. Language such as *"[Security Company] shall not be held liable for any theft or damage to properly resulting from the negligence, or failure to perform assigned duties, on the part of the company or any of its security officers or employees."* is unacceptable and should be reworded by hiring company's legal department to come up with more suitable language that does not leave the company open to liability claims as a result of the contractor's failure to perform.

Corporate Sponsored Events

It is not uncommon for companies holding conferences and expositions to bring proprietary security representatives to oversee and\or augment a venue's contract security provider's staff. This only becomes an issue when the event's contract security provider and the corporation's contract security provider are one and the same. This can happen quite often when dealing with venues that have exclusive security services. The major area of concern is differentiating between the event's temporary security services agreement and the corporation's permanent security services contract. These are two separate contracts and the clauses in them are not interchangeable.

If the company retains the event security provider directly through an existing agreement that provides guidelines for ordering\staffing temporary security details, the clauses in their permanent security services contract will apply to the event. If the event's temporary security services are contracted through the venue or event management company and are totally independent of the corporation's permanent security services contract, then the clauses in the event's temporary security services agreement and the company's permanent security services contract are not interchangeable, even if it is the same security services provider. This is something that needs to be addressed and understood in the very beginning of the event planning process.

Value Added Services

Valued added services are any additional services the contractor may provide in addition to the basic security services contract. These services may include investigations support, consulting services, facility security assessments and emergency incident response support. They may be offered at no additional cost or at a reduced\preferred client rate. Although value added services are not as important as the facility's security service requirements and expectations, they are worth consideration when making the final decision on selecting a service provider.

Chapter 8

Emergency Management & Preparedness

"The only thing harder than planning for an emergency is explaining why you didn't."
~ Unknown

Emergencies can strike anywhere, at any time and with or without notice. Regardless of facility size or location, every facility is susceptible to emergency situations that could potentially place the safety of the site and personnel at risk. These situations could be anything from a routine medical emergency such as a heart attack, to a fire, bomb threat, gas line eruption, earthquake, major storm, or any number of other natural or manmade disasters. Although most companies have emergency action plans in place for immediate response emergency events, an issue oftentimes overlooked in these plans is the potential of severely limited emergency services support when a disaster first strikes.

Many emergency action plans provide short-term facility guidelines to follow until emergency services arrive on site. But what would happen if support could not be provided for days or weeks? If all roadways leading to and from the facility were impassable, blocked by storm debris, fallen trees, floodwaters or 3-4 feet of snow, would the company be able to sustain people trapped at the facility until emergency support could reach the site and provide assistance? How would injured people be treated and cared for?

When developing emergency action plans, it is incumbent on all managers involved in crisis and emergency response management to think outside of the box and include long-term sustainability plans in their overall business continuity and disaster recovery plans. The foundational information and resources provided herein will assist managers in developing comprehensive plans to address most emergency events their facilities may face.

Four very good resources for disaster\emergency management and business continuity programs are:

The *U.S. Federal Emergency Management Agency (FEMA)* Business[13] webpage is by far the best place to start when developing emergency action plans. The website contains a wealth of information and downloadable resources for crisis management program design, management and administration, recovery plans and incident and resource management. Guidelines for plan testing, training and exercise scenarios are also available. FEMA's website also has a media library[14] where site visitors can search for information by keyword, subject, disaster type, category, organization, programs and media type; which are downloadable in audio, document, image and video formats. At the time of this writing there were 22 comprehensive documents covering emergency planning and preparedness, mitigation planning, post disaster recovery and information on FEMA grants and training resources.

U.S. Department of Homeland Security Exercise and Evaluation Program (HSEEP)[15] provides guidance on exercise program management, exercise design and development, exercise conduct and evaluations.

National Fire Protection Association (NFPA®) 1600, Standard on Disaster/Emergency Management and Business Continuity Programs[16] establishes a common set of criteria for all hazards disaster\emergency management and business continuity programs and comprises emergency management and business continuity guidelines for federal and local government agencies, commercial business and industry, not-for-profit and nongovernmental organizations and individual citizens.

Corporate Emergency Access System (CEAS)[17] "…is a turnkey pre-event credentialing program that allows critical business employees to travel through or gain access to restricted areas following a disaster or serious emergency. Credentialing is done through the use of a common identification card recognized by law enforcement and emergency management officials. During times of crisis, businesses and governments rely on employees, contractors, and people with special skills who perform specific functions to help maintain critical operations. When these kinds of essential personnel are prevented from traveling to and accessing their facilities, a domino effect occurs which can cause recovery to grind to a halt. What is often lacking is an effective access control policy and process to help these essential employees and contractors perform their duties."

Emergency Action Plans

Emergency action plans (EAP) are written documents that provide guidance on actions to be taken by companies and workforce members during emergency and disaster situations. As a general rule, EAP's should:

- Identify all potential hazards and risks,

- Identify mitigation strategies and resource requirements,

- Outline cross-functional response teams and responsibilities,

- Provide detailed guidelines on incident management and resumption of business activities, and

- Be reviewed and tested on an annual basis.

The EAP should address all of the "what if" questions about any potential hazards and associated risks a facility could be subjected to. Simply because a company or facility has not experienced any emergencies or a natural disaster has not occurred in a long time does not mean that they will never happen. Just because all systems are working today does not necessarily mean that they will be working tomorrow or after a disaster strikes.

Identifying key stakeholders and conducting brainstorming sessions is the first step in developing a comprehensive EAP. Business unit managers know their area of the business and the adverse impacts a major disaster could have on their operations, personnel and customers. No scenarios or concerns should be summarily dismissed because they may seem too farfetched. There have been instances where a company had a primary and backup emergency generator in place and both generators failed work when electrical power to the facility was lost. When hurricane Katrina struck New Orleans and hurricane Maria struck Puerto Rico, communities and businesses felt the devastating impacts for months, with recovery operations taking years to complete. A train derailment with chemical cars spilling toxic chemicals could very likely lead to a community evacuation. What would the company do if the facility had to shut down all operations and evacuate the community until cleanup was complete and it was safe to return?

As stated, the basic framework of the EAP should include all possible hazards or risks to a company or facility. Typical incidents can be classified into four broad categories.

- Natural Disasters:
  - Severe weather, flooding, forest fire, earthquake, etc.

- Human-Caused Emergencies:
  - Fire, medical, building flooding, workplace violence, security threat, strikes and demonstrations, civil unrest, hazardous material release\spill, terrorism and acts of war.

- Technological Emergencies\Disasters:
  - Utility interruption, network failure, data breach, systems failure.

- Public Health Emergencies:
  - Pandemic, disease outbreak

Drawing from these categories, managers should develop mitigation and response strategies and plans that address facility specific incidents. Areas to be considered are:

- Incident Type -v- Response Team Lead:
  - A facility manager should be the team leader for a power outage or flooding; the security manager should be the team leader for workplace violence; the safety manager should be the team leader for hazardous material spills, etc.

- Business Unit Operations:
  - Facilities, lab operations, vivarium, manufacturing, IT, operations, compliance, etc. What would the impact of each type of event be on a business unit?

After the EAP has been developed and responsibilities assigned, the next step is to ensure all personnel are trained on the plan. This includes the general workforce population and all personnel who are assigned emergency response duties in the plan. Without proper initial and refresher training people may not understand their roles and responsibilities, and what may have looked like a perfectly good plan on paper could fall apart on execution.

EAP Training Guidelines

Training should address all levels within the organization and provide specific guidelines on individual and team roles. The following guidelines provide a broad overview of the types of training that should be provided.

General Workplace Population	• What do in an emergency • Emergency evacuations • Shelter in place • Workplace violence • Emergency commutation\notification system
Emergency Response Teams (ERT)	• All general workforce emergency training • First Aid\AED\CPR certification • ERT roles and responsibilities
Business Unit Managers, Response Team Leaders and Technicians	• All general workforce emergency training • Responsibilities and specific duties to be performed in emergency\disaster incidents. • Incident command team reporting structure.
Incident Commanders (IC)	• Completion of FEMA, DHS, NFPA or local incident commander training. • HAZWOPER training • All EAP sections
Crisis Management Team (CMT)	• Incident command structure • All EAP sections applicable to their role on the CMT • Internal and external communications
Senior Management	• CMT structure • Incident Command Team structure • CMT and IC communications • Their decision making role

The next step in the training process is to conduct drills and exercises to test plan effectiveness and the ability of team members to execute their assigned duties and responsibilities. The best approach for exercise training is a tiered approach that provides gradually increasing levels of complexity that tests the capabilities of teams to successfully implement plan objectives and goals.

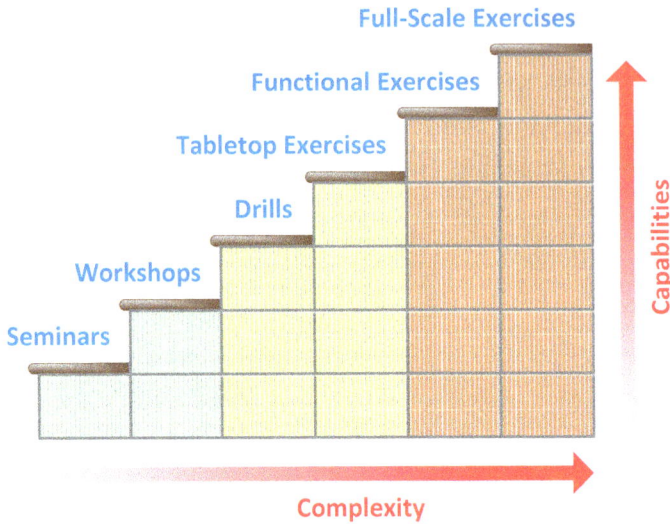

Figure 15: Tiered Exercise Training

Seminars and workshops should be used for plan familiarization and individual\team responsibilities. This method is best used for ERT, business unit and technician initial plan training.

Drills are normally used to test individual and team response to small scale facility specific incidents. A perfect example of this is annual fire alarm evacuation drills. ERT members coordinate floor evacuations and account for personnel at evacuation rally points; security makes emergency notifications and controls building access; facilities personnel operate the fire alarm panel, activating and resetting fire alarms. These types of drills might also include an elevator entrapment, small chemical spill, suspicious package, medical emergency or other such drill.

Tabletop exercises bring together the CMT, incident commanders and team leaders in a classroom type environment to test team response capabilities to larger scale incidents. These may include building flooding, major power outages, explosion, structural collapse, significant hazmat spill and personnel contamination, etc. Realistic scenarios with gradually increasing complexity are developed in advance and participants are required to implement their business unit\team specific actions. Wherever the plan calls for internal notifications, participants should be required to make the phone call and pass on incident information to response teams. When making exercise specific notifications, *the call should always start with "This is a drill. I say again, this is a drill."* If the call recipient is not told that it is a drill, they make think it is an actual emergency. This could result in outside emergency service agencies being notified and responding to what they believe is an actual emergency at the facility, or business unit managers initiating department plans that are not part of the exercise.

Functional exercises are used to test individual business unit and response team capabilities. They are more realistic than tabletop exercises in that all team members and support personnel must implement their EAP as if it were a real incident. If the exercise scenario is for a main waterline break in the building, facilities managers, technicians and operations personnel should be required to implement all response plans as if it were a real incident. The exercise could include a scenario where the water has spread to laboratory or sensitive file storage room, requiring managers of these business units to implement their plans. Calling off duty personnel and asking them how long it would take them to come in if it were a real emergency will give managers a good idea of how long it might take to ramp up to full staffing levels. As previously noted in tabletop exercises, no calls should be made to emergency service agencies and all calls should be prefaced with, *"This is a drill. I say again, this is a drill."*

Full-scale exercises are designed to test the entire facility, campus or company's plans for large-scale emergencies and disasters. There are inherently cross-functional in nature, with most if not all business units and response teams participating in the exercise. Full-scale exercises also require significantly more planning, coordination and resources than other exercises. An example of this type of exercise could be IT testing its backup data center and network redundancy capabilities. Every business unit and system in the company would be affected. IT would need to shut off all connections to the primary network and data center and cut over services to the backup data center. Business unit leaders would need to report when their systems went down, implement their network and system failure action plans and test all systems after they were cut over to the backup data center and again after they are cut back over to the primary data center.

For full-scale exercises involving large scale chemical spills, explosions and active shooter situations, more realism can be added by engaging role players and emergency services agencies. Having victims in makeup to simulate injuries and contamination adds realism to ETR response. Emptying large buckets or barrels of colored water onto an area could be used to simulate a chemical spill; requiring safety and cleanup crews to suit up to contain and clean up the spill. Fire departments, emergency medical services and law enforcement agencies are always looking for places to conduct realistic training in their communities.

Firefighters are always looking for somewhere to practice their hazmat response plans. Hospitals, clinics and ambulance services want to practice their emergency triage capabilities; even if it's just setting up a triage tent and performing onsite emergency medical care. Police departments need places to practice their hostage and active shooter response plans. Including emergency service agencies in full-scale exercises is a great way to add realism to the exercise and build strong corporate-community relations. Emergency service agencies will be more likely to view the company as a partner and in the event of a real emergency or disaster, their response will be much more effective as they already have knowledge of the facility and it's layout from previous exercises at the facility.

It is important to keep in mind that all drills and exercises are training. This needs to be communicated to all employees, managers and contractors. The purpose of the training is to identify plan strengths and weaknesses and make adjustments to improve the organization's emergency response and recovery capabilities. It is inevitable that mistakes will be made somewhere along the line. Managers and participants need to feel comfortable about open discussion of setbacks without fear of retribution from higher level managers. Otherwise things that should be tweaked may go unnoticed until a real emergency incident happens; and the impact could be disastrous.

Security's Role in Emergency Preparedness

Security plays a significant role in emergency preparedness and response activities. More often than not the security phone number is listed as the 24-hour contact number for all facility\company emergencies. Many national and global organizations list an emergency contact number that is answered in the company's security operations center. Once contacted, security coordinates immediate emergency response activates and makes initial incident notifications to designated facility response personnel, emergency service agencies and company management personnel. In major emergencies\disasters, security also serves as the central communications point for all real time information on events as they unfold.

Security cameras at a facility can provide real-time incident monitoring capabilities. The ability to remotely unlock and lock doors allows security to unlock doors for emergency responders or lock down areas within a facility or the entire facility itself in response to emergency conditions unfolding at the facility.

Understanding the critical role security plays in day-to-day business operations and its incident response and support capabilities will help managers develop comprehensive security EAP's. A question that should be asked is, "What would happen if we lost the security operations center or the facility it is in?" A system design approach that allows security to quickly relocate from one facility to another or to transfer operational control to a backup SOC could be the difference that facilitates security program resiliency, or loss or compromise of physical security controls.

Chapter 9

Influencing Corporate Security Culture

"The nature of the relationship between a person and their environment determines their behavior." ~Fritz Perls, 1973.

Contrary to popular thought, the most difficult part of physical security is not designing and building a fully-integrated program to protect assets and personnel. Rather, it is creating a security culture that employees willingly commit to and integrate into their everyday work life that proves to be the most difficult challenge for many security program managers. You can invest hundreds-of-thousands of dollars into the best technology available, develop comprehensive policies and procedures and have emergency actions plans in place to respond to every conceivable threat or risk; but if the general workforce population and senior management don't view and support security as a true priority within the organization, the program may be viewed as nothing more than a necessary evil of doing business; something they only participate in because they have to.

Corporate security culture can be defined as the professional security atmosphere that prevails across an organization and is reflected in the way people perceive and comply with company security protocols. When a secure workplace environment is prioritized and supported within an organization, efficiency will flow in the form of loss reduction and increased productivity. People who believe they are the key to a safe and secure workplace enhance the company's ability to reduce shrinkage and create a safer workplace. When people feel safe in their workplace they are less likely to be concerned for their safety, which in turn allows them to be more productive. When key stakeholders and decision makers prioritize security and see its value to productivity and loss reduction, they will be more likely to support security initiatives and projects.

Influencing corporate security culture is focused on the human or psychological aspect of security; the process of influencing human mentality and behaviors that relate to security and the well-being of other people. Shaping security values and beliefs involves:

- Designing facilities to maintain a secure environment;

- Communicating the importance of security to the workforce;

- Maintaining open lines of communication between staff and leadership;

- Building trust among staff and making them more comfortable with pointing out security issues; and

- Reinforcing security culture and celebrating security wins.

Branding and Marketing Corporate Security Culture

To achieve best results and get staff and leadership to *buy-in* to the corporate security culture, managers must develop and implement effective tools to *sell* the security culture to the *security consumer.* To do this, managers need to take off their operations hat and put on the marketing manager's hat. When security is looked at as an invaluable *service* that a company provides and staff are looked at as *consumers* of that service, the question is in not, "What can I do get people to follow policies and procedures?" But, "How do I package and sell security to my consumer base as something they need and want to buy into?"

Marketing Principles

Human behavior is guided by needs and actions. People may change the way they like to do things, gather information and purchase or buy into something, but their basic psychological needs and philosophical causes of action are two constants that marketers always rely on to sell their products and services. So it stands to reason that the two foundational principles of marketing, Maslow's Hierarchy of Needs and Aristotle's Seven Causes of Human Action[18], would also be effective tools in selling the corporate security culture.

Maslow's hierarchy of needs (*Abraham Maslow, 1943*) is a description of the needs that motivate human behavior. Maslow's theory proposes five different levels of human needs that must be satisfied in successive order for people to achieve their fullest potential. The five needs are:

- Psychological Needs: The basic survival needs of food, water, shelter and rest.

- Safety and Security Needs: The need to feel safe and secure in one's environment.

- Belongingness and Love Needs: The need to belong to a group and develop friendships and intimate relationships.

- Esteem Needs: Prestige and feeling of accomplishment.

- Self-Actualization: Achieving one's fullest potential.

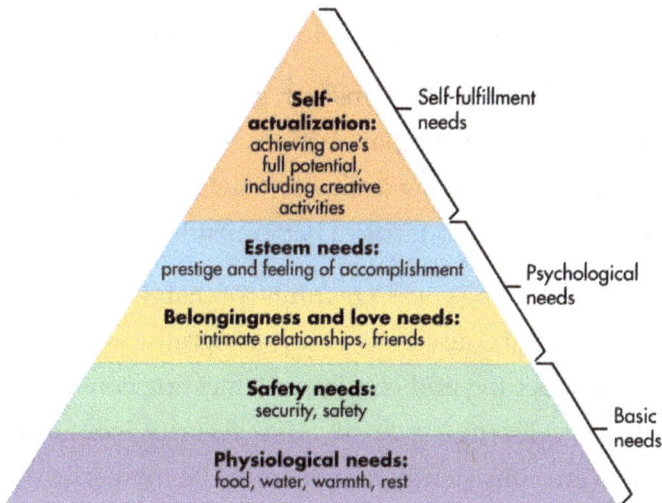

Figure 16: Maslow's Hierarchy of Needs

When we apply these needs to the corporate security environment we find that the right security culture not only satisfies the safety needs, but also has a subconscious and significant impact on the next three needs in Maslow's hierarchy. A person who is issued a company ID badge has undeniable proof that they "belong" to a group (the company) and will undoubtedly develop friendships with other members of that group. When people feel that they are the linchpin is a safe and secure workplace they will be more likely to report security violations and suspicious activities. When their reports are acted on and they are thanked for their actions, they will have a feeling of accomplishment from doing their part in helping to provide a safe and secure workplace. People who feel safe in their workplace are less likely to be concerned for their safety, which in turn allows them to be more productive and achieve their fullest potential.

Greek philosopher and scientist Aristotle wrote that all human actions are rooted in one or more of these seven causes: chance, nature, compulsion, habit, reason, passion, and desire. Aligning security program branding and marketing to one or more of these seven causes is essential to influencing corporate security culture.

1. Chance: Leave nothing to chance. Don't just assume or hope that the security consumer understands what you want them to do and how they should do it. Make sure they understand and that there is no room for confusion.

2. Nature: Human and environmental nature play important roles in motivating consumers to take action. Make sure the actions you tell them to take align with their human nature and the corporate environment.

3. Compulsion: In a world of instant gratification, compulsion causes a significant amount of human actions simply because things can be quickly acted upon. Making it easy for customers to take action and act on their impulses inherently leads to better results.

4. Habit: Human beings are creatures of habit. Although our habitual nature is mostly subconscious, it plays a significant role in how and when we take action. Setting and consistently meeting consumer expectations is critical to developing trust in the security program. If consumer expectations are consistently met they will be more likely to trust security. The more they trust security the more likely they will be to take the desired actions you want them to take.

5. Reason: Reason can be rational or irrational. Rational reasoning is based on logic and weighing possible outcomes. Irrational reasoning is more spontaneous and is usually influenced by stress and negative emotions. Appealing to security consumers' positive emotions is a very effective way to develop a mindset that leads them to make rational decisions; even under stressful situations.

6. Passion: What is the emotional trigger that will motivate a consumer to take action? When the security culture message is crafted and communicated in such a way that it triggers emotion, passionate emotion is triggered. When this happens, it will be almost impossible for a consumer not to take action.

7. <u>Desire:</u> Desire is concerned with feelings, a lifestyle, a personal benefit, or some other tangible or intangible want or need. Understand your audience and communicate with messages and brand statements that position security as a service consumers want and need.

Branding

There is one of two images that immediately pop into the general public's minds when they think of security: strict authoritarians who do not budge or bumbling Paul Blart mall cops who sleep on duty. This is security's public *brand* image. Most of this image is due to how security is portrayed in movies, commercials, cartoons and multimedia, while a lesser portion is also self-inflected. From a very young age children develop images of security from the cartoons they watch and video games they play. The images they remember most are the ones that made them laugh the most. Some may remember that Norman Rockwell drawing of the elderly security officer with a clunky *Detex®* clock around his neck, feet propped up on a desk and sound asleep. Movies like *Paul Blart: Mall Cop®* do nothing to help the image either. On the other hand, security also has a number of self-inflicted wounds that they wholly own. With the advent of social media there are hundreds, if not thousands of images of overly aggressive security officers or security officers sleeping on duty. Security contractors who hire and assign security officers with marginally acceptable appearance and minimal interpersonal communications and reasoning skills do little to help the image either.

As you can see, brand integrity is a very fragile thing. In order to influence security culture and achieve program buy-in, security program manager's need to build and brand a professional corporate security program that dispels the negative impressions people may have developed over a lifetime of somewhat less than positive input. Once that brand is developed, care needs to be taken to ensure the security program image remains professional, that security consistently meets company and worker needs and expectations, and that security can always be counted on, even in the most stressful of times. Too many slips and you could easily find yourself having to recover from a sleeping mall cop image.

You may have noticed by now that the terms Security Guard and Security Guard Company are shied away from in this book. Rather, the terms security officer and security provider have been used throughout. It's an image thing. Changing how we describe security is the first step in changing how we view security.

A well branded security image is one that builds relationships and coveys the message that:

- Security is a professional business partner;

- Security cares about me;

- Security begins with me; and

- I have a responsibility to report suspicious activities, security breaches and policy noncompliance.

If your branding and imaging convey these four messages, you will have a security culture that workers believe in and appreciate, and one in which workers become an extension of the security department.

Selling the Security Culture

Sales is a give and take process where people exchange one item of value for another item of value. I have something you want or need and you have something I want or need. Based on our perceived value of the item, we may purchase or trade something we perceive to be of equal value for that item. We do this every day in the purchases we make at a store or online and in the interactions we have with other people. When raising children we exchange something of value with the child in exchange for a desired behavior or achievement. In a new relationship we try sell ourselves to the other person as the one person they have always been looking for. When looking for a new job, well sell ourselves to the perspective employer as the person who best fits the position requirements and can get the job done. If hired, the employer will pay us in both salary and benefits for the work that we do.

Selling the security culture is no different. The typical company security sales model tells workers what they must do in the workplace – wear their badge; sign in and escort visitors; you can park here but not there; report suspicious activity and behavior – and the worker is expected to comply with company security guidelines. Workers who do not follow security guidelines could also be subject to disciplinary actions. Sure, this may work for security awareness purposes, but it does nothing to get people to willingly buy into the security culture. The problem with this model is that it's a one-way transaction. To achieve true security program buy-in, workers need to receive something of value in exchange for buying into the program. Some may think that having a safe and secure workplace is what the worker gets in return. But this doesn't go far enough. Real return on investment comes when security answers the consumers' question of "What's in it for me?", and then delivers tangible and intangible products and services that meet the consumer's wants and needs.

Program Packaging and Sales Opportunities

Packaging is all about how security's products and services are branded and the materials and tools used to sell the security culture. Packaging that engages and captures the attention of the consumer will have them wanting to buy into what is being sold and coming back for more. Packaging that is bland and repetitive will leave consumers bored and wondering when the sales pitch will end. They may buy into what is being sold, but only because they have to; not because they want to. An example of both models is provided on the following pages.

These are numerous opportunities to influence corporate security culture throughout an organization. The first being New Hire Orientation (NHO). NHO is the best opportunity to present the corporate security culture to new employees and onsite contractors.

- It is your initial security culture "market pitch";

- The first impression of security that will be remembered throughout a person's employment; and

- Has the greatest impact on future security compliance.

The security presentation should be dynamic, informative and engaging and should

- Cover company security protocols;

- Identify security's role;

- Tell worker's what role they play;

- Answer the question, Why is security important to me?; and

- Offer people resources that can help them provide for their and their family's safety and security outside of the workplace. (What's in it for me?)

You never know who might be sitting in on the NHO presentation; employees, contractors, managers, directors or vice presidents of departments; nor who might be going to the security page for personal security information. It might be the new purchasing manager with responsibility for your business unit, a security conscious business unit manager, a decision maker with responsibility for approving projects for your department.

The following pages contain two examples of security NHO presentations. The first is a typical presentation given in many organizations; the other a rebranded presentation. The difference between the two is actually quite stark.

Typical Security NHO Presentation

SECURITY

- Access Control
  - Everyone entering the building must have a company issued ID badge
  - The badge must be worn at all times while on company property
  - The card reader function of the badge allows you access though card reader controlled doors
  - DO NOT tailgate or allow others to tailgate
  - DO NOT lend your badge to anyone else to use
  - If you need access to a restricted area, send an email to security@mycompany.com
  - If you lose your badge, immediately notify Security at ext. 2222 to have the badge turned off.
    - A new badge can be obtained at the Security Office
    - Badging hours are Monday – Friday, 8:00 am – 5:00pm

SECURITY

- Visitor Access
  - Visitors must be signed in at the building lobby
  - Visitors must be escorted at all times while on company property
  - In the event of a building evacuation, take your visitor with you to your evacuation rally point
- Property Control
  - Company property can not be removed from the building without a manager's approval
  - Have your manager send an email to security@mycompany.com authorizing you to remove the property. The email must contain
    - A description of the property, including make, model and serial number
    - Date and time the property is being removed
    - Reason for removal
    - Expected date and time property will be returned (if any)

SECURITY

- Parking
  - Parking is provided for employees and contractors in lots A & C
  - Lot B is for visitor parking only. <u>DO NOT</u> park in this lot.
  - <u>DO NOT</u> park in handicap parking spaces without a state issued handicap license plate or handicap tag
    - Temporary company handicap tags can be obtained from security
    - Send an email to security@mycompany.com with the reason for the request and the expected time of temporary disability or medical condition
      - <u>DO NOT</u> provide detailed information on medical condition
      - Describe condition in general terms (i.e. recovering from injury, pregnant, etc.)
    - You may be required to provide a doctor's note

SECURITY

- Emergency Procedures
  - Emergency Evacuation
    - Walk, <u>DO NOT</u> run, to the nearest fire exit door and leave the building and go to your designated evacuation rally point
    - <u>DO NOT</u> reenter the building unless the "<u>ALL CLEAR</u>" is given by the Fire Department, Facilities, Safety or Security
  - Fire
    - Pull the nearest fire alarm pull station
    - Alert others in your immediate area
    - Follow Emergency Evacuation Procedures
  - Medical Emergency
    - CALL 911 – <u>DO NOT</u> hang up
    - Notify Security at ext. 2911
    - Provide medical assistance if trained to do so

SECURITY

- Report Suspicious Activities, Persons and Items
  - If you see something, say something
  - Unusual or out of place packages or items
    - <u>DO NOT</u> touch or move the item
  - People loitering on the property or around the building
  - People looking into car windows
  - Notify Security at ext. 2222

Reflecting back on the recommended presentation guidelines previously discussed, does this presentation:

- Cover company security protocols? Yes.

- Identify security's role? Not really.

- Tell worker's what role they play? Somewhat so; with a lot of DO NOT's and MUST do's along the way.

- Answer the question, Why is security important to me? No.

- Offer people resources that help them provide for their and their family's safety and security outside of the workplace? No.

- Was it dynamic, informative and engaging? Not even close.

It would not be a stretch of the imagination to say that most people didn't even read through all of the slides for this presentation. Some may have even asked themselves, why am I reading this? And therein lays the rub. If this is the type of presentation currently in use at your company and you don't like it, why would you continue to use it? Now let's look at a rebranded presentation.

Rebranded Security NHO Presentation

What does this cover slide say about security? If your answer is that a safe and secure workplace is a team effort and that you and Security are partners on the same team, you already understand how packaging and imaging play a big role in perceptions. If your first image tells people you and they are on the same team, they will want to learn more about this team and their role on it.

Now let's look at the other slides.

Corporate Security Principles

- Provide a safe and secure work environment for company employees, contractors and visitors
- Implementation of security strategies that provide for the protection of company personnel, assets and information
  - Security polices & procedures
  - Electronic physical security systems (access control & CCTV)
  - Partnering with employees and onsite contractors
  - Security awareness training
  - Access to security information through the company security portal page (www.security.mycompany.com)
  - Response to emergency conditions\situations

Oppaset Security Consulting: Advancing Security Solutions for Today's Business Needs

Security's Role

- Lobby Reception
  - Access Control
  - Visitor Management
- Safety & Security Patrols – 24/7
  - After-hours escorts throughout the campus
  - Building patrols
  - Incident response
  - Employee assistance
- Security Command Center
  - Security and building\lab systems monitoring
  - Emergency Response
- ID Badges
  - General Access
  - Restricted Area Access

Oppaset Security Consulting: Advancing Security Solutions for Today's Business Needs

Your Role

YOU

ARE AT THE 🔒 CENTER OF

SEC🔒RITY

YOU ARE THE FOUNDATION OF THE COMPANY'S SECURITY CULTURE

- Your security awareness and partnership are the most significant contributing factors to a safe and secure workplace
- Know and follow company security policies and procedures
- Take an active role in ensuring compliance with safety and security guidelines
- Report incidents and things that just don't seem right to security
- If you are unsure of something, ask Security

Building Access

- People with ill intent look and dress just like you
- Wear your badge at all times
  - It's the only way we know that you work here
- Report lost or stolen badges to Security immediately
- Never loan your badge to another person; or use another person's badge
- Prevent piggybacking and tailgating

"It's not always easy to pick the one that doesn't belong."

Visitor Access

- All visitors must sign in and be escorted at all times while on company property
  - Employment Candidates
  - Business partners
  - Sales representatives
  - Regulatory inspectors
  - Meeting\event guests
  - Family members and friends
- Anyone 18 years or older will need to present photo identification
- In the event of an emergency evacuation, take your visitors with you to your designated evacuation rally point.

Oppaset Security Consulting: Advancing Security Solutions for Today's Business Needs

Information Security

- Use strong passwords
  - Never share your username or password with anyone
  - IT will never ask you for your password
- Never download files or software that you were not expecting
- Be wary of phishing emails
  - No subject
  - Misspellings and grammatical errors
  - Telling you you need to do something, or else
  - Offering you something that sounds too good to be true
- Do not leave company laptop or information in the passenger compartment of your vehicle
- Report laptop and company cellphone theft to Security immediately

Oppaset Security Consulting: Advancing Security Solutions for Today's Business Needs

In the Event of an Emergency

- Know what to do in an emergency
  - Emergency Action Guides are posted in meeting rooms and kitchenettes
- Every fire alarm is real
- Be familiar with your building and evacuation routes
  - Nearest stairwell and exit door
  - Evacuation rally point
  - Take visitors with you
  - Follow ERT & Security Instructions
- Do not use elevators
- If you observe an emergency, immediately notify Security (ext. 2911) and stay on the phone

Medical Emergency

- Know what to do in an emergency
  - Emergency Action Guides are posted in meeting rooms and kitchenettes
- Immediately notify Security (ext. 2911) and stay on the phone
- Call 911 if it is life threatening
- Assure victim help is on the way
- Perform CPR\First Aid if trained to do so.
- Enlist others to help keep pathway to victim clear for emergency responders.
- Provide assistance to security and emergency responders if requested to do so.

Active Shooter

- Remain focused and aware of your surroundings
- Call Police (911) and Security (2911)
- **RUN:**
  - Leave area and building by safest and quickest route
  - Take others with you
- **HIDE:**
  - Go to shelter-in-place location
  - Lock or block door
  - Put cellphone on vibrate
  - Remain in shelter until police arrive
  - Do not rush police, keep your hands over your head and follow all instructions
- **FIGHT:**
  - If you have to fight, the violence of your actions might save your life and the lives of others

Things That Don't Seem Right

- Suspicious activities and persons
  - People loitering outside the building or in parking areas
  - Someone looking in cars
  - Suspected drug use or transactions
  - Unidentified people in work area
  - Elicitation attempts
- Suspicious Items
  - Items that are out of place (backpack, box, luggage, duffle bag, etc.)
  - Parcels with excessive postage, misspellings and\or inappropriately addressed
  - Leaking parcels or suspicious odor
  - Do not handle suspicious items
  - Firearms or other weapons
- Notify Security immediately

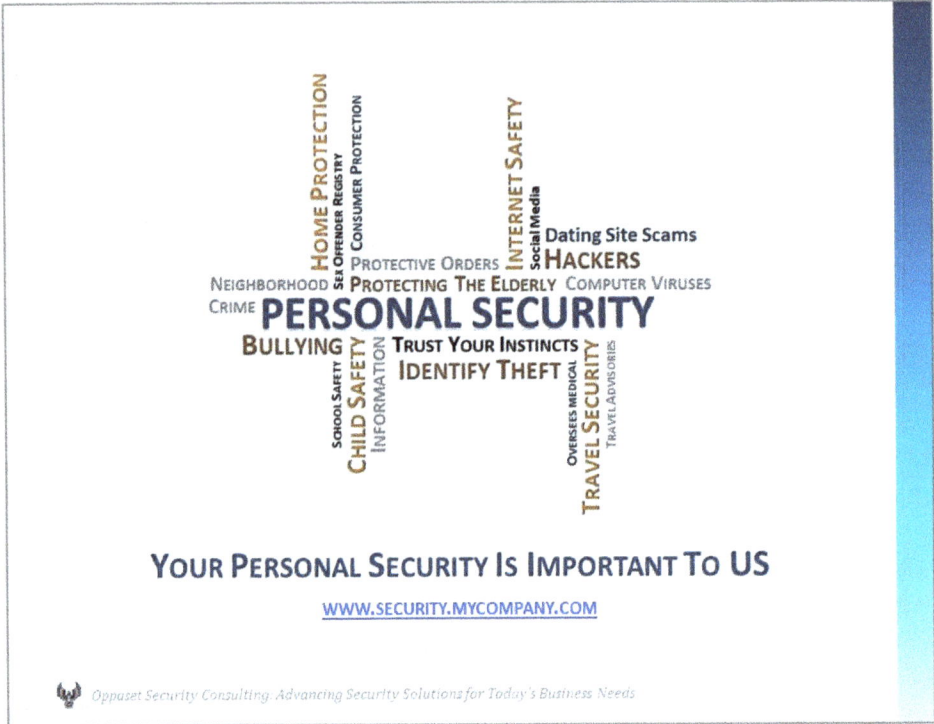

Before moving on to the Security Portal or Intranet page, we should take a break to review the how the security culture was presented in the rebranded Security NHO presentation. The rebranded presentation is colorful and uses a lot of images. This is done because illustrations have the ability to attract attention, aid retention, enhance understanding and create context. The Your Roll slide tells people that they are the linchpin in the corporate security culture and are the most significant factor in a safe and secure workplace. We can't do it without you. The image of the clown in the group in the Access Control slide subconsciously imparts the message that, I'm not a clown; that's why I wear my badge. And, as we move on to the conclusion of the presentation, we wrap it up by telling the consumer that their personal security is important to us. We care about the personal safety and security of you and your family.

Click on the Security Portal page link on the last slide and up pops the company's internal security page.

An often underutilized resource for security information and messaging is the company's intranet portal page. Although a lot of companies have a security portal page, it is not all that uncommon that there is no Security link on the company's main page. Many times the link to the security page listed on the page of the parent department security reports to: Facilities, Safety, HR. When the security link is not on the main page, users normally type security in the search bar find the link. After clicking on the security link, they are taken to security's page. One would thing that with the important role that security plays in workplace safety, security and emergency response that the link to the security page would be in a prominent location on the company's main employee facing portal page. This is not to say that companies don't value security's role in the organization. What if the reason the security page is buried on another page is because the Security page hasn't *earned* its place on the company's main page?

Most security pages contain information on company security policy and procedures: how to get a badge, report an incident, parking and visitor procedures. There may be a link to a medical advice and traveler assistance service provider if the company uses a vendor who providers these services. But there is usually little else on the page. As with the typical Security NHO presentation, if you've seen it once there's usually little desire to go back and see it again.

With the amount of personal safety and security information in online resources, community and state resources, security news articles and periodicals, the Security page could be the best one stop shopping resource for employees seeking personal safety and security information. Imagine if an employee was looking for information on identify theft, frauds or scams because of something that happened that they were suspicious of, or had concerns about bullying or online child safety. They may not know where to go for information, but they will probably remember that during the Security NHO presentation they heard that security had a portal page with personal safety and security information. They go to the page and find what they're looking for and may start doing further research from there. Now imagine that the last thing that you do during the NHO presentation is open the Security, give a brief overview of the information available and then close out with a review of the Child Safety Tips page. If that doesn't get people to buy into the corporate security culture, nothing will. You've provided a professional presentation, shown the security consumer what you have to offer them personally and the last thing they remember you saying is that you cared about them and their children.

The following pages contain sample Corporate Security pages for consideration.

My Links ▼   Art Crow ▼

Emergency Number
Ext. 2911

Emergency Action Guide

Welcome To Corporate Security
Partnering For a Safe & Secure Workplace

Security Officer of The Month!

Jane Hernandez

Congratulations Jane Hernandez! Jane was selected as the June 2017 Security Officer of the Month. Jane has been a member of our security team for 3 years and is the day shift patrol officer. You may have seen her ...read more

If You See Something, Say Something

Suspicious activities, persons and items can pose a real threat the company and our workforce. Use the following link to report an incident or anything that just doesn't seem right. ...Report an Incident

You can also call Security at ext. 2222

June is Internet Safety Month: Learn how to Protect Your Children Online

With school out and summer upon us, our children will have more time on their hands and more opportunity to engage in social media and other online activities. It is also a time when they may be more susceptible to online predators, and an important time to talk to our kids about online safety. A somewhat difficult conversation can be much easier if you have the right resources. ...read more

Security News & Trends

Security Magazine, June 27, 2017 – Department of Homeland Security (DHS) Announces Enhanced Security Measures for International Flights. "The new policies will be implemented in phases. DHS said, and will affect 180 airlines in 105 countries — and about 2,000 flights and 325,000 passengers per day." ...read more

Security Magazine, June 27, 2107 – Most Americans Say They Are Prepared for an Emergency or Disaster. "A report from Princeton Survey Research Associates International shows that two thirds of U.S. adults feel they would be prepared if an emergency or disaster struck their community today, including 20 percent who say they would be very prepared." How prepared are you? ...read more

Corporate Safety & Security Teams Participate in Citywide Disaster Exercise

June 15, 2017 – Members of the corporate Safety & Security teams participated in a joint citywide disaster drill to test coordinated community and business response to a natural disaster. ...read more

Read Archived Security News & Tips! Security Tips| News

Security Policy & Practices
Physical Security Policy
Physical Security Standards
Restricted Area Access
  – Submit an Access Request
Visitors
  – Preregister a Visitor

Identification Badges
Report a Lost or Stolen Badge
Get a New Badge
Request a Contractor\Vendor Badge

Information Security
IT Security Policy
Phishing and Social Engineering

Travel Security
International SOS
Travel Advisories

Personal Security
Child Safety
Home Protection
Fraud & Scams
Identify Theft
Security Tips & News
Helpful Links & Phone Numbers

Security Contacts
Your Security Team

My Links ▼   Art Crow ▼

Search Security Tips

Child Safety Tips

Online Child Safety
Parent Resources
Online Learning Games

School Safety
Grade School
High School
College

Bullying

Drugs

Guns

Stranger Danger

Security Policy & Practices
Physical Security Policy
Physical Security Standards
Restricted Area Access
  – Submit an Access Request
Visitors
  – Preregister a Visitor

Identification Badges
Report a Lost or Stolen Badge
Get a New Badge
Request a Contractor\Vendor Badge

Information Security
IT Security Policy
Phishing and Social Engineering

Travel Security
International SOS
Travel Advisories

Personal Security
Child Safety
Home Protection
Fraud & Scams
Identify Theft
Security Tips & News
Helpful Links & Phone Numbers

Security Contacts
Your Security Team

Read Archived Security News & Tips! Security Tips | News

My Links ▼   Art Crow ▼

Search Security Tips

Child Safety Tips

Online Child Safety

The opportunities kids have to socialize online come with benefits and risks. Parents can help reduce these risks by talking to kids about making safe and responsible online decisions.

Some Alarming Statistics:

- One of every 17 minors online has been threatened or harassed online.
- An alarming 75% of children share personal information about themselves willingly over the Internet in exchange for goods and services.
- 20% of U.S. teens who regularly log on to the Internet have received a sexual solicitation or approach over the Internet, 1 in 33 have been aggressively pursued sexually online.
- 77% of youths are contacted by online predators by age 14, and 22% of children ages 10 to 13 are approached.
- Only 25% of our children will tell a parent about an encounter with a predator who approached or solicited sex while on the Internet, and less than 10% report sexual solicitation to legal authorities.
- Only 1/3 of online households in the United States proactively protect their children and teens by using filtering or blocking software.

Following are links to some very useful information that will help you become more aware of the extent of this issue and provide you with a host of resources for keeping your children safe online.

US Federal Trade Commission - Protecting Kids Online

A wealth of information on cyberbullying, social media, computer security, mobile phones texting and sexting, and online predators.

FBI Parent Resources

Get advice and information to help protect your children from the dangers lurking in both the online and offline worlds.

McGruff Just for Kids

Online safety games for kids. Bullying, community safety, school safety, guns, drugs and online safety.

NetsmartzKids.org

Run by the National Center for Missing & Exploited Children, NetSmartz for Kids provides age appropriate information for children ages 5 – 17. Videos of the month are submitted by children and featured on the site's main page.

Read Archived Security News & Tips! Security Tips | News

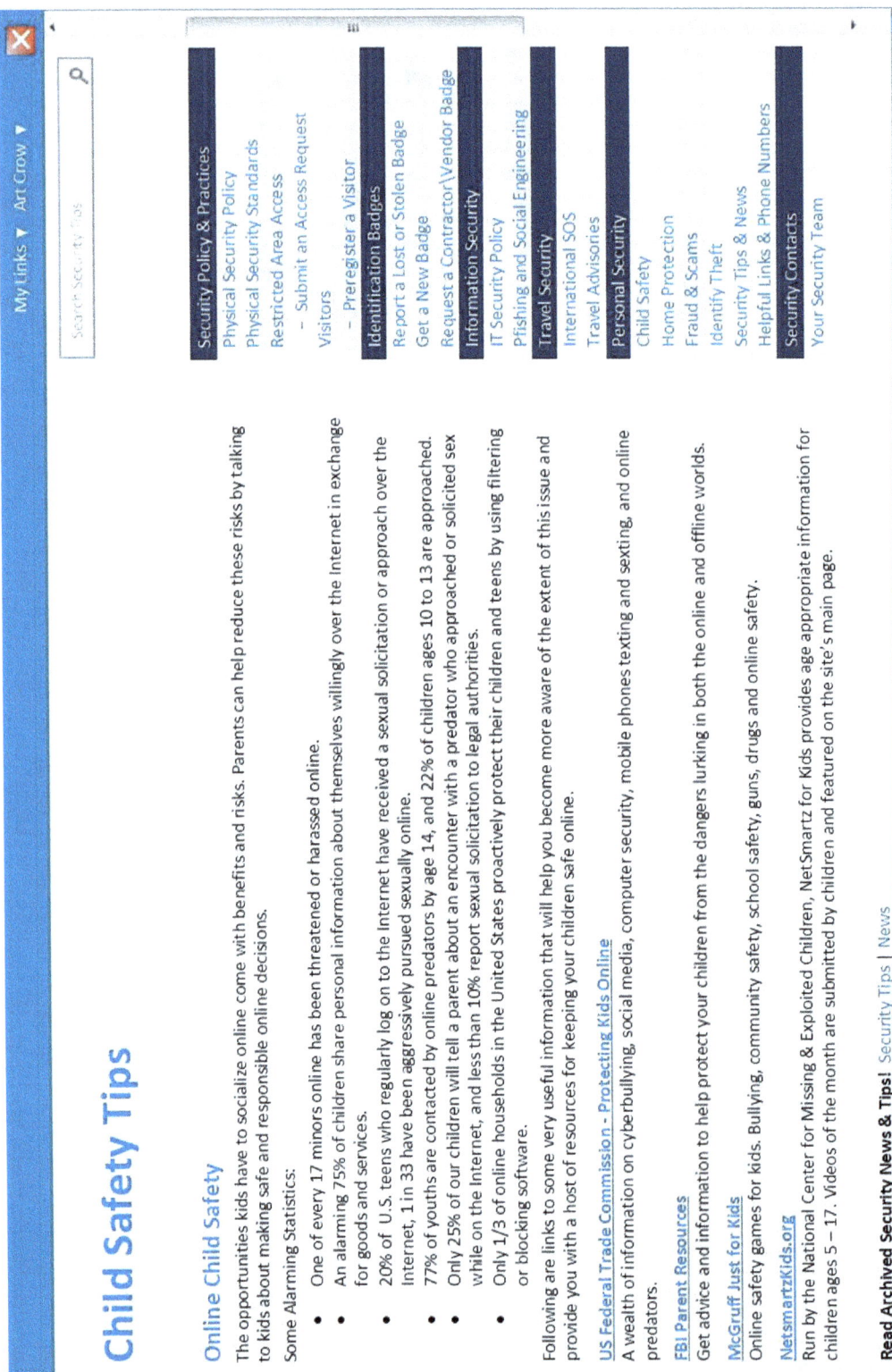

Security Policy & Practices
Physical Security Policy
Physical Security Standards
Restricted Area Access
  – Submit an Access Request
Visitors
  – Preregister a Visitor
Identification Badges
Report a Lost or Stolen Badge
Get a New Badge
Request a Contractor\Vendor Badge
Information Security
IT Security Policy
Phishing and Social Engineering
Travel Security
International SOS
Travel Advisories
Personal Security
Child Safety
Home Protection
Fraud & Scams
Identify Theft
Security Tips & News
Helpful Links & Phone Numbers
Security Contacts
Your Security Team

At first glance it may seem like a lot of work to build and maintain this type of company security page, but it's really not all that difficult. The page layout will need to follow company intranet layout guidelines, so how the page will look from a design layout perspective is already a given. Page content, how the page feels and how user friendly it is is a different story. Seeking out assistance from the company's marketing and corporate communications departments can prove invaluable in when designing page content and feel.

There are a number of key elements in the sample corporate security pages provided that should be considered when designing a company security page.

Emergency Phone Number

The emergency phone number (extension) and link to the company's emergency action guide are in bold red text to the upper right of the page. The red text and having the information at the top of the page (left or right) draws the user's attention to it, making it easier to locate in an emergency.

Content Information Links

All links to content information (policy & procedure, badge requests, personal security, security contacts, etc.) are contained in one column on the page. These can be links that take a user to downloadable PDF documents or other security pages with more information and resource links; like the Child Safety Tips page.

Security Wins

Once a month there should be an article about a security win. This is important as it tells users something good about security. If a member of the security staff receives an award, this is a great way to recognize that person with a short article on them and their award. Other articles for consideration are successful completion of a security program audit, security actions that led to the discovery of a major water leak, prevented a theft or led to the arrest of persons responsible for vehicle break-ins or theft from company property; recognizing a non-security employee who did something that contributed to workplace safety and security; or an interview with a senior manager on their philosophies on workplace safety and security.

If You See Something, Say Something

This should be displayed prominently on the page and provide the security phone number and a link to report an incident. The link can either open the user's new email window where they can report the incident via email, or it can link to an anonymous incident reporting application if the company uses such an application.

Security Tip of the Month

Tips of the month can include child safety, seasonal weather safety, holiday safety, identify theft, frauds and scams, etc. Wherever possible, monthly tips should align with any recognized monthly awareness initiatives: June is national internet safety month; March is fraud awareness month. All that's needed is the article heading, 2 – 3 sentences that provide an overview and a link to further information. The link could take users to another security page with the relevant information or link to an external article or resource website.

Security News & Trends

This section should focus on useful external news articles about security information and trends. The US Department of Homeland security announcing increased security measures for international flights is useful information for business travelers and people making vacation plans. An article focusing on research findings on personal disaster preparedness may make people think of emergency preparedness plans for them and their families. As with the security tip of the month, these should be monthly articles with a few sentences that provide an overview and a link to the external resources.

Ideas for resource content are almost limitless. Following are some examples of information that many people may find useful.

Information Security

- IT Policy
- Malware\Spyware
- Laptop Security
- Pfishing
- Suspicious Emails

Personal Security

- Home Protection
- Travel Security
- Identity Protection
- Scam Alerts
- Emergency Preparedness

Child Safety

- Online Safety
- Bullying
- Stranger Danger
- Home Emergencies
- School Safety

Security Tips & News

- Seasonal Safety Tips
- Security in the News
- Company Security News
- Security Events
- Personal\Child Safety Tips

Helpful Links

- US State Department Travel Advisories
- Ready.gov
- Consumer Protection Agency
- Sex Offender Registry

Phone Numbers

- Police & Fire Department Nonemergency
- Battered Women's Shelter
- Rape Crisis Hotline
- Suicide Crisis Hotline

Security Team

- Senior Manager
- Security Command Center
- Emergency Number
- Security Posts
- Security Staff

Department Contacts

- Safety
- Facilities
- IT Security Operations
- Ethics Hotline
- Business Continuity

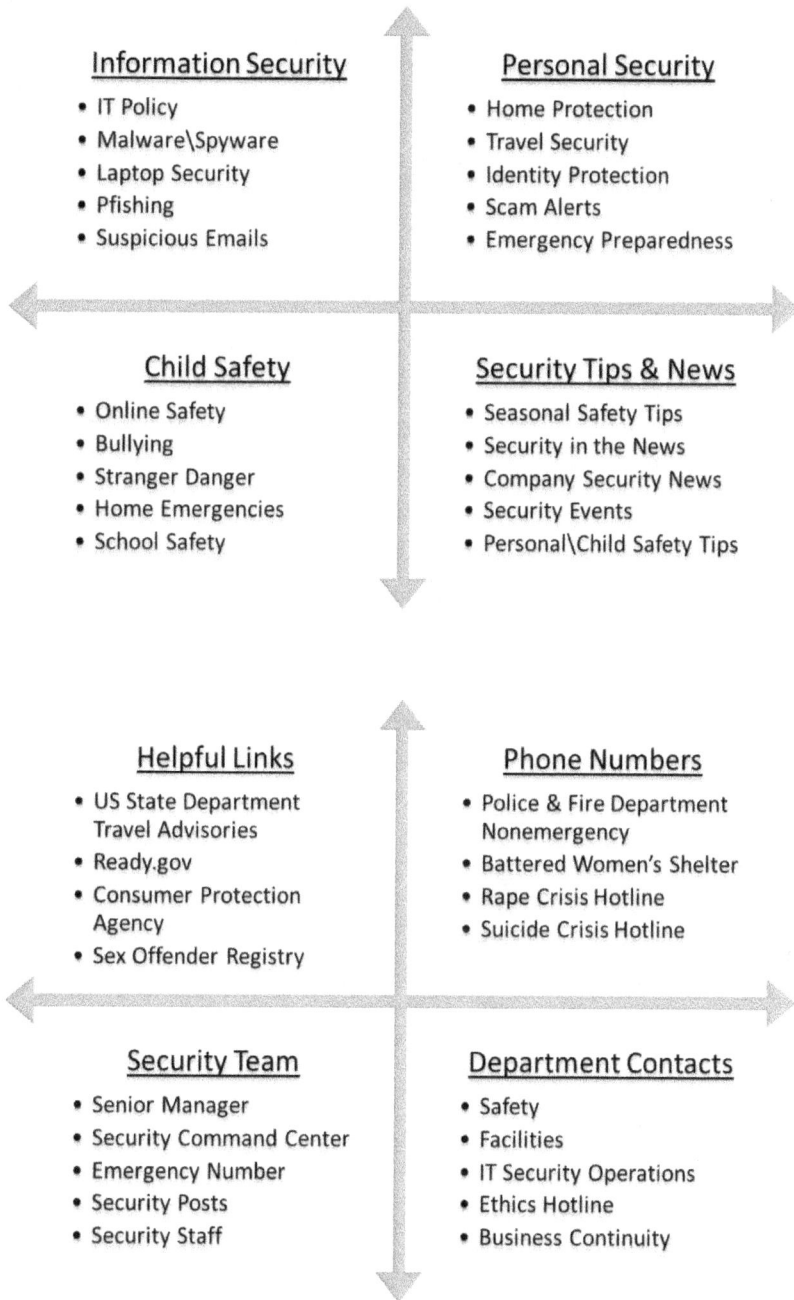

Influencing corporate security culture is an ongoing process that requires relationship building, consensus building and a continuous process improvement approach. Accomplishing this requires:

Consistency

Regardless of the facility or where it is located, the security experience is the same. Each facility should have the same policies and procedures; enforcement of security guidelines is the same; even the security officer uniforms should be the same.

Collaboration

Management by walking around. The people who work at the facility, and especially senior management, need to know who the site security manager or lead is. Interacting with people in their workspaces and engaging in casual conversation with them builds relationships and trust. It is not uncommon during a casual walk around of the facility that a worker might point out a door they noticed that was not closing properly, or share information on an incident or suspicious activities they may not have otherwise reported. Attending business unit department meetings and lunch & learn sessions keep lines of communication open between security, business unit leaders and their teams. Giving a security presentation and answering security related questions during a lunch & learn session is a great way to build strong relationships.

Market Research and Continuous Improvement

Conduct annual or semiannual employee security surveys to get a feel of how the workforce perceives security. What do they believe are security's strong points and weak points? What are their security concerns?

- Seek to answer the question, "What can we do to make the security experience better?"

- Share survey results and any security concerns and recommendations you have with management.

- Make improvements where they can be made and where they won't have a negative impact on the facility's overall security posture.

Exploit Opportunities That Create A Positive Security Image

Host a Child Safety Day that includes games and activities. Have a raffle with safety related prizes. Many police and fire departments have child safety related programs they like to share with the community. The police department might set up a bicycle safety course in the parking lot and provide child identity kits.

The fire department might talk about fire safety and let kids climb into a fire truck or ambulance. The first time a child is injured and has to be transported to the hospital can be a very scary experience. Having gone into an ambulance at the child safety day event and learning what's in it can go a long way in reducing the child's stress level; especially if they're being transported to the hospital and a parent isn't with them.

Get involved in company community service days. Security officers working alongside other employees on community service day builds relationships and shows that security cares about the community.

Participate in fundraising drives; company sponsored or other. If the company has an annual craft fare where portions of the proceeds are donated to charity, set up a table and sell all lost and found items that haven't been claimed during the year. Set yard sale prices and barter and trade. If someone comes up and notices an item they believe they had lost earlier in the year, give them the bargain-basement deal, $1.00 - $2.00. After all, all proceeds from the lost and found property sale are going to charity.

Implementing some or all of the recommendations in this chapter will go a long way in developing a positive security image and creating a corporate security culture where workplace safety and security are at the forefront of everyone's mind.

Chapter 10

Measuring Security Value

Quantifying Security Expense –v– Security Value

Physical security has historically been viewed as a non-revenue generating business operating expense. Since security is not a revenue producing business unit, the biggest stumbling block most security program managers' face when developing security budgets is quantifying the value security provides to the company. Whether it is for annual security operating or project budgets, the question is always the same. What is the return on the investment (ROI)? We know that security helps prevent loss of company property and that it also helps to increase worker productivity, but how do we express that in dollars and cents? Using the Cost-to-Recover formula outlined in Chapter 2 we can show return on investment for protection of assets and revenue saved whenever an asset is recovered. As a recap, to determine cost to recover, we simply need to divide the loss value by the company's after-tax net profit:

$$\frac{Loss\ Value}{ATNP\ \%} = Cost\ to\ Recover$$

Using this formula we can show a return on investment dollar value in terms of additional profit required to recover from a loss event. If a company with a 4.35% ATNP experiences a loss of two laptop computers with a total estimated value of $3,500 (including the laptops, software and provisioning costs), the additional revenue required to recover the cost of replacing those two laptops is $80,460.

$$\frac{\$3,500}{4.35\ \%} = \$80,460$$

If the argument is that the company has an insurance policy that covers losses due to theft and property damage, applying the same formula to the insurance policy deductible can show additional revenue that would be required to recover from the deductible if it were paid out. Let's assume the company has a $5,000,000 policy that includes a theft and property damage rider. Since business insurance providers normally require a minimum 1% - 2% deductible on all business policies, we'll assume the company's deductible rate is 1.5%; $75,000.

$$\frac{\$75,000}{4.35\ \%} = \$1,724,138$$

This means the company will have to generate $1.7 million in additional profit to recover from a loss before the insurance company pays $1.00 on a loss claim.

A company's ATNP % plays a significant role in actual costs to recover from a loss event. The lower the ATNP %, the higher the cost will be; the higher the ATNP %, the lower the cost will be. Following is a comparison of cost to recover from the same $75,000 deductible at a 4.35% and 7.90% ATNP rate.

4.35% ATNP	**7.90% ATNP**
$$\frac{\$75,000}{4.35\ \%} = \$1,724,138$$	$$\frac{\$75,000}{7.90\ \%} = \$949,367$$

With this formula it is easy show security investment value. For every $1.00 invested in security, the ROI in potential (or actual) revenue savings is $13.00 - $23.00; or a 1,300% - 2,300% ROI. Investing $500,000 or more annually on physical security for a facility with millions of dollars in assets now becomes a fiscally responsible business investment, as opposed an expense line item that does not contribute to company profits.

Security's impact on workplace productivity is a bit more ambiguous and more difficult to quantify as there are no definitive studies focusing on the link between workplace security and its impact on stress reduction and productivity. Although there are many studies on the impact of stress on productivity, with statistics and recommendations on workplace design, lighting, plants, furniture, worker compensation and fitness, there have been no similar studies that show a correlation between physical security and productivity. What we do know from studies conducted by the U.S. Center for Disease Control, American Institute of Stress and the Stress Management Society is that a reduction in workplace stress can increase productivity between 5% - 15% and decrease worker errors by up to 70%. Although physical security impact data is not available, we can safely assume from existing data that any reduction in stress achieved by providing a safe and secure workplace will inherently have a positive impact on productivity and reductions in human error.

Company image and security start at the front door. The *"Face of the Company"* that prospective customers, existing customers, visitors and auditors first come into contact with when they enter the building lobby is the receptionist or security officer sitting at the lobby desk. That person's appearance, professional demeanor and how they control building access is the first on-site impression of company operations that will be instilled in the person's mind; and one which will inevitably remain with them during their site visit and set the tone for everything that follows thereafter. Professional appearance and demeanor convey an image of professionalism and attention to detail. A less than professional appearance and demeanor could convey an image of lackadaisical business operations and little attention to detail. Even something as simple as an unkempt reception desk or lobby could convey a message of disorganization.

If the visitor is a prospective customer, this could be one of the factors that could make or break a deal if the difference between what the company and a competitor are offering is razor thin: When we visited company X, the lobby was sharp and we were treated like royalty from the moment we entered the door. When we visited company Y, the receptionist didn't have it together and it took a long time to get signed in and for the receptionist to notify our host. If the visitor is an executive from an existing customer company where security image and culture are very important, that executive might wonder why they are doing business with a company that does not share the same security philosophy. If it is a compliance or regulatory auditor or team, the audit began the moment they walked in the door. Good appearance, demeanor and access control means the audit will go as planned. If it is not a good first impression, the auditors might be left with an image of confusion and disorganization. An otherwise routine audit might very well turn into a more detailed examination of policies, procedures and processes. A minor deviation that may have otherwise received a notice of noncompliance and require documented proof of changes made to meet compliance guidelines could very well turn into regulatory fines. If it is a customer audit, contractual penalties could be imposed, including loss of any contractual bonuses.

Security Metrics

As with all business metrics, security metrics should provide quantifiable measurements than can be used to track and assess both the qualitative and quantitative value of the security function. To accomplish this, security metrics should set measureable and achievable business goals that address performance, benchmarking and financial goals that align with overall company business goals and objectives. Many security metrics fall short of this mark as they are usually focused on day-to-day security duties and activities (how many visitors were processed, how many and what type of incidents were reported, how many tours of the facility were conducted). While this is useful information that should be reported on, a metrics report that relies solely on this type of data does not communicate security's real value to the organization.

Performance

Performance can be measured in terms of security processes, day-to-day security activities, how well the security service provider is meeting contractual guidelines and how they impact security's ability to meet overall business risk reduction strategies and enhance the customer experience. The metric should identify performance expectations and how well those expectations are being met.

Examples of these are:

Facility Security Tours:

- What is the minimum number of tours required per shift per day?

- Were all tours completed or were some only partially completed?

- What were the contributing factors that lead to insufficient or incomplete tours and what is being done to improve tour performance?

- If a deviance or emergency situation was identified during a tour, what was it and how was it handled? If it was a major water leak or other such event that caused damage, what was the loss value of the damage and what could the loss value have been had security not identified the issue when they did? A ½ inch above ceiling water supply line broke and caused $25,000 in damage. Had security not discovered the leak when they had, water could have spread to other areas of the building, which could have in resulted in $100,000 or more in damage.

Security Incident Reports:

- How many and what types of incidents did security respond to?

- Where were the incidents? Facility, location in building?

- Are incidents trending up or down?

- If thefts are being reported, what is being done to reduce theft incidents rates? For company property, what was the value of the theft? If property was recovered, how much did the recovery contribute in profit savings? If security prevented the left of a laptop computer valued at $2,500, security saved the company a potential $57,471 in lost profit to recover from the theft.

Security Provider Performance:

- What are the key deliverables in the security service contract?

- If all security personnel are required to be trained in First Aid\CPR\AED, how many are trained? How does this equate to security's ability to respond to medical emergencies? If 80% of personnel are trained\certified, this means that security medical response capability is only operating at 80% efficiency. What is being done to bring staff up to required training levels?

- If the security provider is required to ensure a minimum 95% staffing level, is the staffing level being consistently met? What impact has the staffing level had on overtime, contactor employee retention and ability of the contractor to fill all required security posts?

- Random audits of service provider and subcontractor personnel records can show whether or not they are meeting minimum pre-employment screening and training requirements.

Customer Service:

- Internal customer satisfaction surveys can provide invaluable feedback on employee and contractor perceptions of security performance and value to the company.

- On a scale of 1 – 5: How personable are security officers? Does the receptionist greet you when you enter the facility? How responsive has security been to your inquiries and requests? How would you rate security's overall value to the company? If you could add or change one thing that might enhance the security experience or provide a safer or more secure work environment, what would it be?

- What is security's overall rating? Are there any areas that need improvement? How do current survey results compare to past results?

- If enhancement recommendations have been made, are they reasonable and can they be implemented? What would the cost be to implement process or systems changes? What security and general workforce training would need to be developed and how would it be delivered?

Benchmarking

Benchmarking goals should align with company goals and objectives, as well as industry benchmark standards.

- If the company has a goal of increasing operational efficiency or that all employees and contractors complete a training program by a specified date, is security on track to meet these goals?

- If the company's industry shrinkage or theft rate is 3%, what is the facility's shrinkage rate? Is it above or below the industry average? If above industry average, what are the root causes and what is being done to reduce shrinkage? What investments need to be made to achieve these objectives?

- If security provides the operator call function and the company has a call center or help desk call center application, applicable security phones should be connected to the application to monitor incoming call service. Metrics on how many calls are answered per hour, call wait time and dropped call rates can be measured against industry call center averages or the company's customer service center benchmarks.

Financial

Are security expenditures in line with quarterly and annual budget projects? Is security on target to meet budget guidelines? Identify factors that have contributed to over expenditure, or efficiencies implemented that have helped to reduce quarterly and annual spend. Are security projects on target to meet budget and timeline expectations? Will there be costs overruns? How will project timelines that are not met impact the overall project schedule and other business units? What cost savings will be realized if the project is completed before the project's projected completion date?

These are just a few examples of security metrics that can be used to measure the qualitative and quantitative value of security operations and security's overall value to the organization. Collaboration with other business unit managers can help managers develop other metrics that address specific risks associated with a particular business unit's operations.

Chapter 11

Industrial & Economic Espionage

Understanding the Threat

It is no secret that businesses spy on their competitors to gain a strategic market advantage and governments spy on businesses to gain information that will enhance the militaries and economies of their countries. It is also no secret that as the global marketplace has expanded and competitiveness for market dominance has increased, so has the quest by corporations and governments to obtain insider information on business.

The U.S. Federal Bureau of Investigation[19] estimates the losses to U.S. companies as the result of trade secret theft at somewhere between $25 billion and $100 billion, while the U.S. International Trade Commission[20] estimates annual losses are closer to $300+ billion. Other estimates place the annual cost to U.S. businesses at $500+ billion.

Trade secret theft is universally defined by law enforcement and government intelligence agencies as:

- *Corporate\Industrial Espionage*: The theft of trade secrets that occurs when someone knowingly steals or misappropriates a trade secret to the economic benefit of anyone other than the owner.

- *Economic Espionage:* The theft of trade secrets that occurs when a trade secret is stolen for the benefit of a foreign government, foreign instrumentality, or foreign agent.

While the majority of media coverage about trade secret theft revolves around theft through information systems hacking, there have also been numerous instances of physical items such as laptop computers, company R&D blueprints and documents, manufacturing and processing concepts, and prototype equipment being stolen from a company's premises.

When it comes to the types of people who steal company secrets, it is estimated that 60% - 80% of trade secret theft is committed by current or former employees, contractors or business partners. A corporate spy or mole could be a company manager, engineer, scientist, maintenance technician, cleaner, security officer, an inspector or anyone who has legitimate access to the facility. A person's motivation for stealing corporate secrets could be feeling disgruntled about the company or their job, personal financial problems, drug or alcohol addiction, or blackmail. There is also the real possibility that the person could be an *intelligence professional* skilled in obtaining classified government and corporate secrets.

Since the end of the Cold War a number of countries, including some of America's closest allies, have refocused a large percentage their intelligence gathering capabilities to obtaining proprietary information from American corporations. There are also a number of former government intelligence operatives and employees who have transitioned to *spies-for-hire* after leaving their government intelligence jobs. Some have started their own private intelligence consulting agencies, while other work for such companies as Orbis Business Intelligence™, Elite Security Holdings™, Fusion GPS™ and other such companies. There is even an association for *corporate intelligence professionals;* Strategic Competitive Intelligence Professionals (SCIP)[21]. This is not to say that SCIP is an association of former intelligence agents or that any of its members or member companies engage in unethical means to collect business intelligence information. But when a number of its members are also members of the Association of Former Intelligence Officers (AFIO) who offer business intelligence services that provide *"intelligence deeply rooted"* at the global and local levels of organizations, one has to take seriously the skill level of the corporate intelligence professional and their ability to acquire company trade secrets. Case examples of trade secret theft provided by the FBI on its website include:

- October 2017: Former Chemours employee charged with conspiracy to steal trade secrets in connection with plan to sell trade secrets to Chinese investors. Former employee intended to infringe on Chemours' lucrative sodium cyanide business.

- July 2017: Businessman indicted for allegedly stealing employer's trade secrets while planning for new job with rival firm in China.

- May 2017: Chinese National Pleads Guilty To Economic Espionage And Theft Of A Trade Secret From U.S. Company.

- May 2017: Seven People Charged With Conspiring to Steal Trade Secrets For Benefit of Chinese Manufacturing Company. Case Involved Dual-Use Technology With Military Applications.

- August 2016: Local chemical engineer must pay approximately $4 million in restitution for unlawfully possessing trade secrets. The former employee used the trade secrets to start his own business.

- May 2015: Two Chinese professors were among six defendants charged with economic espionage and theft of trade secrets in connection with their roles in a long-running effort to obtain U.S. trade secrets for the benefit of universities and companies controlled by the People's Republic of China (PRC).

- January 2015: A computer science engineer was sentenced for stealing sensitive trade secrets from a trading firm in New Jersey and a Chicago-based financial firm.

- July 2014: A California man was sentenced to 15 years in prison on multiple economic espionage-related charges in connection with his theft of trade secrets from DuPont regarding its chloride-route titanium dioxide (TiO2) production technology and the subsequent selling of that information to state-owned companies of the PRC.

- May 2014: Five Chinese military hackers were indicted on charges of computer hacking, economic espionage, and other offenses directed at six victims in the U.S. nuclear power, metals, and solar products industries.

The threat of industrial and economic espionage is real and can have a significant negative impact on a company's profitability and consumer, business partner and stockholder confidence; making it incumbent on security program managers to implement sound security protocols to combat the threat.

Social Engineering

In the context of security, social engineering refers to the psychological manipulation of people into performing actions that violate established security protocols or persuade them into divulging confidential information. Identity thieves use social engineering to get people to provide personal information; sales representatives use social engineering to get through to decision makers; a terminated employee or contractor may use social engineering to gain access to the building; corporate intelligence professionals use social engineering as one of their tools to steal company trade secrets.

Kevin Mitnick, arguably one of the best computer hackers of his time, is credited with hacking into dozens of corporate and government computer systems spanning a 19 year period from the time he was 13 until his capture in 1995. In 1995 Mitnick was charged with 14 counts of wire fraud, 8 counts of possession of unauthorized access devices, interception of wire or electronic communications, unauthorized access to a federal computer, and causing damage to a computer. In his 2002 book, The Art of Deception, Mitnick states that he compromised computers solely by using passwords and codes that he gained by social engineering. In some instances he would talk to the administrative assistant for an executive manager and claim to be a person working on an important project with a tight deadline. He would then request information on how to get hold of a person working on the project so he could get some critical information he needed to meet the project deadline. Once he had the contact information, he would then call the person and tell them the executive's administrative assistant gave him their name to help him get the information he required. If the person wanted to call the admin first to get verification, the admin would invariably tell them that Kevin was on the project team and he\she referred Kevin to them. The rest was just a matter of following this method until he was able to get the access and information he was seeking.

Another example of social engineering is recounted in the following true story.

"One morning a few years back, a group of strangers walked into a large shipping firm and walked out with access to the firm's entire corporate network. How did they do it? By obtaining small amounts of access, bit by bit, from a number of different employees in that firm. First, they did research about the company for two days before even attempting to set foot on the premises. For example, they learned key employees' names by calling HR. Next, they pretended to lose their key to the front door, and a man let them in. Then they "lost" their identity badges when entering the third floor secured area, smiled, and a friendly employee opened the door for them.'

'The strangers knew the CFO was out of town, so they were able to enter his office and obtain financial data off his unlocked computer. They dug through the corporate trash, finding all kinds of useful documents. They asked a janitor for a garbage pail in which to place their contents and carried all of this data out of the building in their hands. The strangers had studied the CFO's voice, so they were able to phone, pretending to be the CFO, in a rush, desperately in need of his network password. From there, they used regular technical hacking tools to gain super-user access into the system.'

'In this case, the strangers were network consultants performing a security audit for the CFO without any other employees' knowledge. They were never given any privileged information from the CFO but were able to obtain all the access they wanted through social engineering."

This story was recounted by Kapil Raina, a security expert and co-author of mCommerce Security: A Beginner's Guide, based on an actual workplace experience with a previous employer.[22]

While Mitnick used social engineering to talk people into providing him with usernames and passwords to gain access to electronic files, the story about how the two network security consultants gained access to company files and the network shows that social engineering is also an effective tool for gaining physical to facilities.

The Company Man: Protecting America's Secrets

A very good case study on how industrial\economic espionage unfolds is the FBI's video The Company Man: Protecting America's Secrets.[23] The video recounts the case of two Chinese businessmen who attempted to steal RIS Insulation Systems' trade secrets. Three very important questions that were asked and answered in the text accompanying the video, and which are very important when considering facility security are:

- **What social networking sites did the subjects use to target the company employees and how did they use the information they learned?**

  The subjects used LinkedIn and Facebook to spot and assess employees working at the target company. They then used a "headhunter" as a proxy to see which employees might be interested in leaving their positions.

- **After being turned down for the proposed joint venture, how soon did they attempt to trespass at the plant?**

  The two subjects waited four days, then departed the corporate headquarters area and flew to a rural town across the country where the manufacturing plant was located. Upon arrival, they checked into a local hotel. In the evening, they attempted to access the plant without authorization for the first time.

- **Did the subjects actually walk into the plant despite being denied a tour?**

  Yes. The company denied the subjects' initial request to visit the manufacturing plant. Undeterred, the subjects traveled over 500 miles directly to the rural plant. The subjects entered the plant in the evening and took their own self-guided tour, taking photographs until challenged. Their initial pretext was they were looking for a gas station. They returned the next day and were found in the employee parking lot watching employees enter and exit the plant. When confronted, the subjects advised they were looking for a fishing lake nearby. Since the plant was located in a small rural town, the factory doors were left unattended.

The big takeaway form this video is: A determined industrial\economic espionage operative will stop at nothing to steal a company's trade secrets. Including bribing employees with large sums of money or walking in through an open door and gathering whatever information they can. Even manufacturing plants in rural communities are not immune to professionals seeking to steal a company's trade secrets. Company managers should endeavor to learn as much as they can about identifying attempted or actual trade secret theft and reporting it, as well as implement proactive security measures to reduce risk and protect confidential and proprietary company information from theft.

When a Theft Becomes More Than Just a Theft

It is not uncommon for medium sized and large companies to experience some form of workplace theft. Cellphones come up missing, money and personal items are stolen from workstations or desk drawers, and company laptops, equipment and materials are also stolen. While such theft is not uncommon, it is important to be able to draw a distinction between what might be random theft as opposed to a theft that might indicate a potential espionage related incident.

Most random theft comes and goes in spurts. There may be a few days or weeks where personal items and maybe even a few laptops are stolen. In these types of incidents, thefts are usually from multiple areas within a facility on the same day. If there are laptop thefts, there will usually be 3 – 5 laptops stolen from one area or from different floors within the building. This is because the opportunist nature of the common thief is to grab as much stuff as possible from an area before moving on to the next or leaving the facility. It's all about grab and go before they get caught. While these incidents pose a real threat to workplace security and need to be addressed immediately, a more concerning theft is when one or two items of high importance are stolen. Although the first reaction may be to treat all workplace theft as just theft, certain types of theft should cause managers to consider the bigger picture of potential trade secret theft. Examples of these include:

- A prototype turbo charger is stolen from an engine manufacturer. A review of video footage shows that an employee took the turbo charger and put it in his vehicle. It is also known that this employee was having personal financial difficultly. While the thought may be that the turbo charger was stolen to be turned in for scrap metal money, the bigger question is why was the prototype stolen and not any other metal items that may have been readily available? Surely an employee working in a plant with prototype equipment should have known that the theft of a prototype would draw more attention than the theft of something else that was not so critical to the company's R&D process.

- A laptop computer and lab notebook are stolen from a scientist or engineer's workstation. If the person who committed the theft had to walk past numerous workstations with unsecured laptops, why did they bypass all of the other laptops that could have been stolen and take that particular laptop *and* the lab notebook?

- Engineering or process blueprints are reported missing and a search of the facility and files results in them not being found, or they are found at a copy machine. If they were found at the copy machine and the person who reported them missing said that they had not copied the documents and is insistent that they had left them at their workstation at the end of the previous day, who copied them and why?

- An employee or contractor is found at a general use computer workstation and system logs show that the person attempted to access confidential electronic files using a generic username name and password; such as training login credentials used during software training sessions.

The one thing all of these incidents have in common is: Something just doesn't seem right with each theft or attempted theft. If something of high corporate intelligence value is stolen or a person's behavior just doesn't add up, chances are it could be much more than just simple theft or a minor lapse in the person's judgement. And, although incident follow up may not lead to confirmation of trade secret theft in all cases, identifying even just one trade secret theft incident could save a company millions, if not billions in annual revenue.

Protecting Company Secrets

Business unit managers and senior leadership should identify company information that might be valuable to competitors and that if stolen could have a negative impact on the company and\or its employees. These include:

- Corporate strategies
- Marketing and new product plans
- Manufacturing and processing schematics
- Target markets and prospect information
- Plant closures and new plan development
- Product designs and proprietary formulas
- Corporate partner and contract agreements (delivery, pricing, terms)
- Customer and supplier information
- Merger and acquisition plans
- Financials, revenues, P&L and budgets
- Marketing, advertising and packaging expenditures
- Organizational charts, staffing levels and wage\salary rates
- Personnel records

Information Classification

An information\document security policy that assigns classification levels and provides guidelines on document\information use, handling and storage should be developed. Document classification should be content based, with weight given to the subject matter in a document or system. Whenever a document contains information that meets more than one classification level (i.e., Confidential and Internal Use Only), the higher classification should apply to the entire document. Whenever a company is performing government related work, the government information classification should take precedence over any business document classification. Examples of business information classifications include:

- **Confidential:** Highest information classification level. Theft or unauthorized release of information would very likely have a significant negative impact on the business and its competitiveness. Documents in this classification may include corporate strategies, product designs and proprietary formulas, R&D information and manufacturing and process schematics.

- **Restricted:** Medium information classification level. Theft or unauthorized release of information would likely have a moderate negative impact on the business and its competitiveness. Documents in this classification may include plant closures and new plant development plans, workforce restructuring plans, corporate partner and contractor agreements.

- **Internal Use Only:** Lowest internal classification level. Theft or release of information would likely have a negligible or no impact on the business or its competitiveness. Documents in this classification may include department organizational charts, staffing levels, internal phone directories and staffing levels.

- **Public:** Information that is generally available to the public and has no restrictions on information sharing.

Protection Strategies

While sound IT\Network security practices and the use of antivirus and antimalware software serve to protect information from hackers, physical security controls inhibit physical access to information systems and other sources of company information. The following recommendations will help to restrict unauthorized physical to company information and assets.

- Implement building access controls, such as those outlined in the previous chapters that restrict building access to only authorized personnel and their authorized visitors. Require all visitors to be escorted at all times.

- Sensitive documents should be kept in locked filing cabinets or drawers when they are not in use.

- Sensitive information and systems should be kept in card access controlled areas that require approval before card access is granted.

- Institute a clean desk policy. No sensitive company information should be left on desks at the end of the work day.

- Erase all whiteboards that contain strategy, process design, formulas or other sensitive proprietary information. If information is required for future use, a picture should be taken of the whiteboard before it is erased and the image placed is a secure document folder.

- Do not discard sensitive documents in the trash or recycle bins. Purchase crosscut document shredders or engage the services of a document shredding company to shred all documents and media (compact disks, etc.), including drafts that are no longer needed. If using a shredding service, all shredding should be conducted on site and a trusted employee should observe the shredding process.

- Work with meeting\event planning staff to provide security for all offsite company meetings. Access to offsite meetings should be restricted to company personnel and their authorized guests only. At the conclusion of meetings, meeting areas should be swept for any company information that may have been left behind.

- Lock dumpsters and place no trespassing signs on them. Dumpster diving is a common tactic used whereby someone digs through a company's trash to find useful or sensitive information. Except where prohibited by local law, dumpster diving is not illegal. In the 1988 Supreme Court Ruling in California vs. Greenwood, the court ruled that when a person throws something out, that item is now in the public domain. If a no trespassing sign is placed on the dumpster, a person removing items from the dumpster could be charged with unlawful trespass or trespassing.

- Company badges should not have the company name or logo on them. If a badge is lost or stolen, anyone who has possession of the badge will know what company it is for and will be able to gain card access to the facility. Use a multicolored bar code or other distinguishing mark that can be used to identify it as a company badge.

- Company badges should have a picture of the badge-holder on them that is large enough so it can be recognized by security and other company personnel. As people age or badge pictures wear down, new badge pictures should be taken and\or new badges issued.

- Develop an employee and contractor security awareness program and ensure all onsite personnel are trained in information and physical security policies and procedures. Provide monthly security awareness articles on the company intranet page.

- Treat all security procedure violations as serious violations of company policy. All violations of network and physical security protocols should be followed up on. Repeated violations of company security policies and procedures should result in disciplinary actions, up to and including termination of employment.

- Report actual or suspected trade secret theft to the FBI's local field office.

As stated at the beginning of this book, absolute protection is impossible to achieve in most environments. Regardless of facility design, security systems deployed and security staffing levels, a determined intruder with the appropriate skills, resources and motivation can gain access to almost any facility. The goal of physical security is to implement reasonable measures to reduce the likelihood of an adverse event occurring.

Appendix A

Facility Protection Measures

The concepts in this appendix provide baseline guidance on physical security levels of protection that should be considered when developing facility security plans. The information provided is by no means all-inclusive for all facility types. Regulatory and\or certification requirements may dictate higher levels of protection based on a company's business model. Facilities involved in certain federal government work may be required to have doors that meet minimum tooled entry resistance specifications. A drug manufacturing facility may be required to install large vaults for bulk storage of drug compound processing materials and finished product.

The security budget is also a factor in determining which approaches a company may take in securing their facilities. The higher the security measure, the more expensive it will be to implement. A card reader with a PIN pad usually costs twice as much as a standard card reader. A card reader with a thumb print reader can cost as much 5 ½ times more than a standard card reader. With the advancements in IP camera technology, IP cameras are only slightly more expensive than analog cameras. Regulatory requirements may also require a company to maintain recorded video for 90 – 180 days, which in turn increases the cost for storage servers.

Knowledge of the company's regulatory\certification security requirements and how much leeway there is in the budget for physical security protection measures play equally important roles in determining which measures can be implemented. For planning purposes, wherever the following recommendations call for a PIN pad card reader, the PIN pad card reader may be substituted for a standard card reader if there are no regulatory\certification requirements that specifically call for dual factor authentication for access.

Definitions:

CR: Card reader

CCTV: Closed circuit television camera

DECB: Delayed egress electric crash bar

DRB: Door release button (required for all doors equipped with MAG locks)

DSM: Door sensing mechanism (door contact)

ELM: Electric mortise lockset

ETH: Electric transfer hinge

GB: Glass break sensor

MAG: Electromagnetic lock

ML: Mortise lockset

PCR: Card reader with PIN pad. May be substituted with biometric reader.

SDR: Local alarm annunciator

Area\Door Type	Protection	Access Level
Perimeter Personnel Doors	CR, ELM, DSM, RTE, ETH, CCTV. Staffed with receptionist\security officer whenever unlocked.	General
Perimeter Egress Only Doors	DSM, DECB, SDR, ETH, CCTV. Staffed with receptionist\security officer whenever unlocked.	N/A
Building Lobby *Sample layouts at Figures 15 & 16*	CR, MAG, DSM, RTE, DRB, CCTV w\views of Lobby doors and reception desk. Staffed with receptionist\security officer whenever unlocked.	General
R&D and QA Labs	Dual factor authentication, PCR, ELM, DSM, RTE, ETH, CCTV,	Restricted
Legal File Storage Room	Dual factor authentication, PCR, ELM, DSM, RTE, ETH, CCTV	Restricted

Area\Door Type	Protection	Access Level
QA\QC File Storage Room	Dual factor authentication, PCR, ELM, DSM, RTE, CCTV, ETH	Restricted
Manufacturing\Processing	CR, ELM, DSM, RTE, CCTV, ETH	Restricted
Critical Infrastructure (HVAC, Electrical, etc.)	Dual factor authentication, PCR, ELM, DSM, RTE, CCTV, ETH	Restricted
Fire Command Center	ML	Restricted Keyway
Data Center	Dual factor authentication, PCR, ELM, DSM, RTE, CCTV, ETH	Restricted
Main Distribution Field (DMF)	Dual factor authentication, CR, ELM, DSM, RTE, ETH, CCTV	Restricted
Intermittent Distribution Field (IDF)	CR, ELM, DSM, RTE, ETH, CCTV	Restricted
Loading Dock Exterior Door *Sample layout Figure 17*	CR, ELM, DSM, RTE, ETH, CCTV	Restricted
Loading Dock Interior Doors	CR, ELM, DSM, RTE, ETH, CCTV	General
Loading Dock Overhead Door	DSM, CCTV	N/A
Loading Dock Office	CR, ELM, DSM, RTE, ETH, CCTV	Restricted
Hazardous Material Storage Rooms	CR, ELM, DSM, RTE, ETH, CCTV	Restricted
First floor windows	GB	N/A

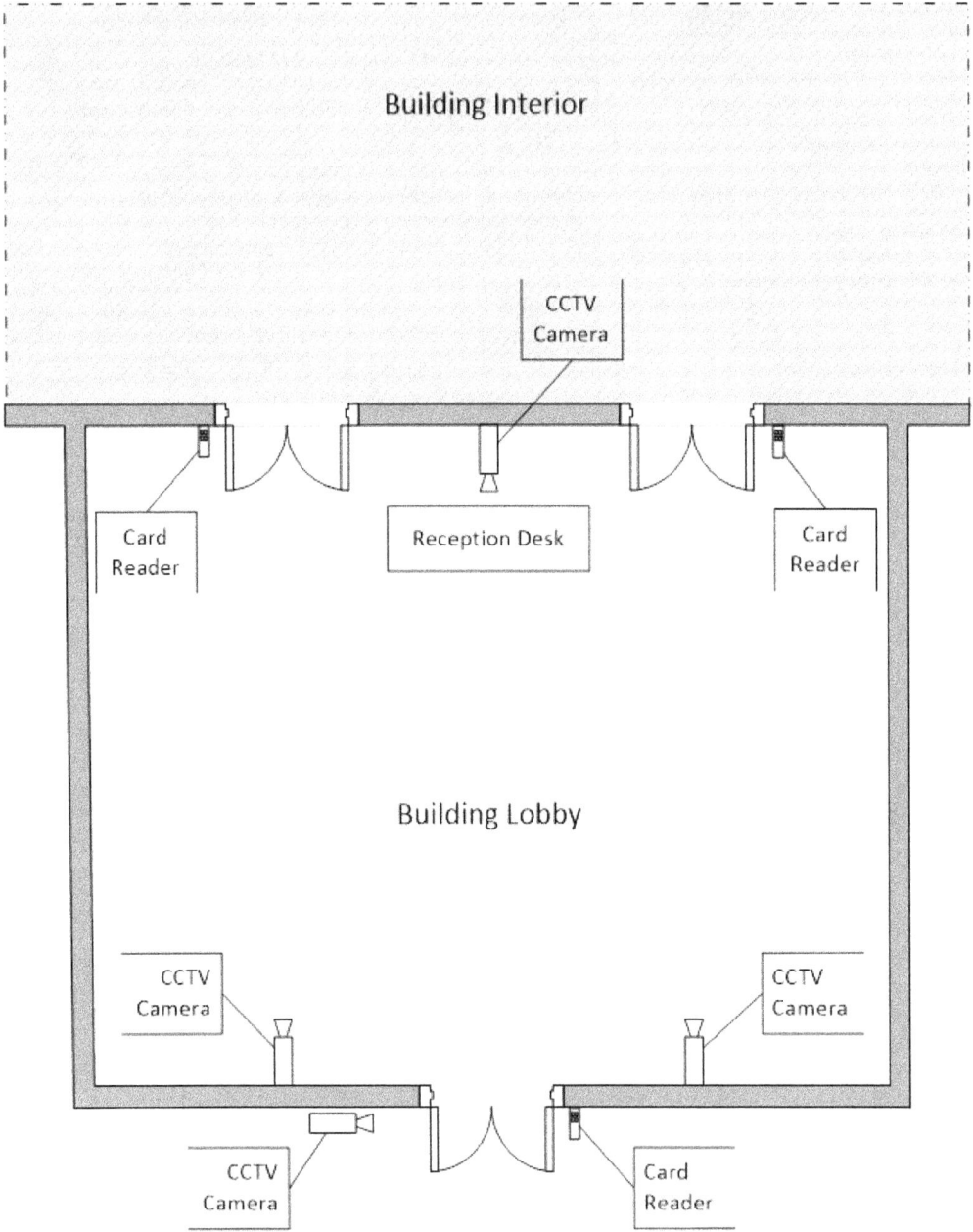

Figure 17: Sample Building Lobby Layout – A (Not to Scale)

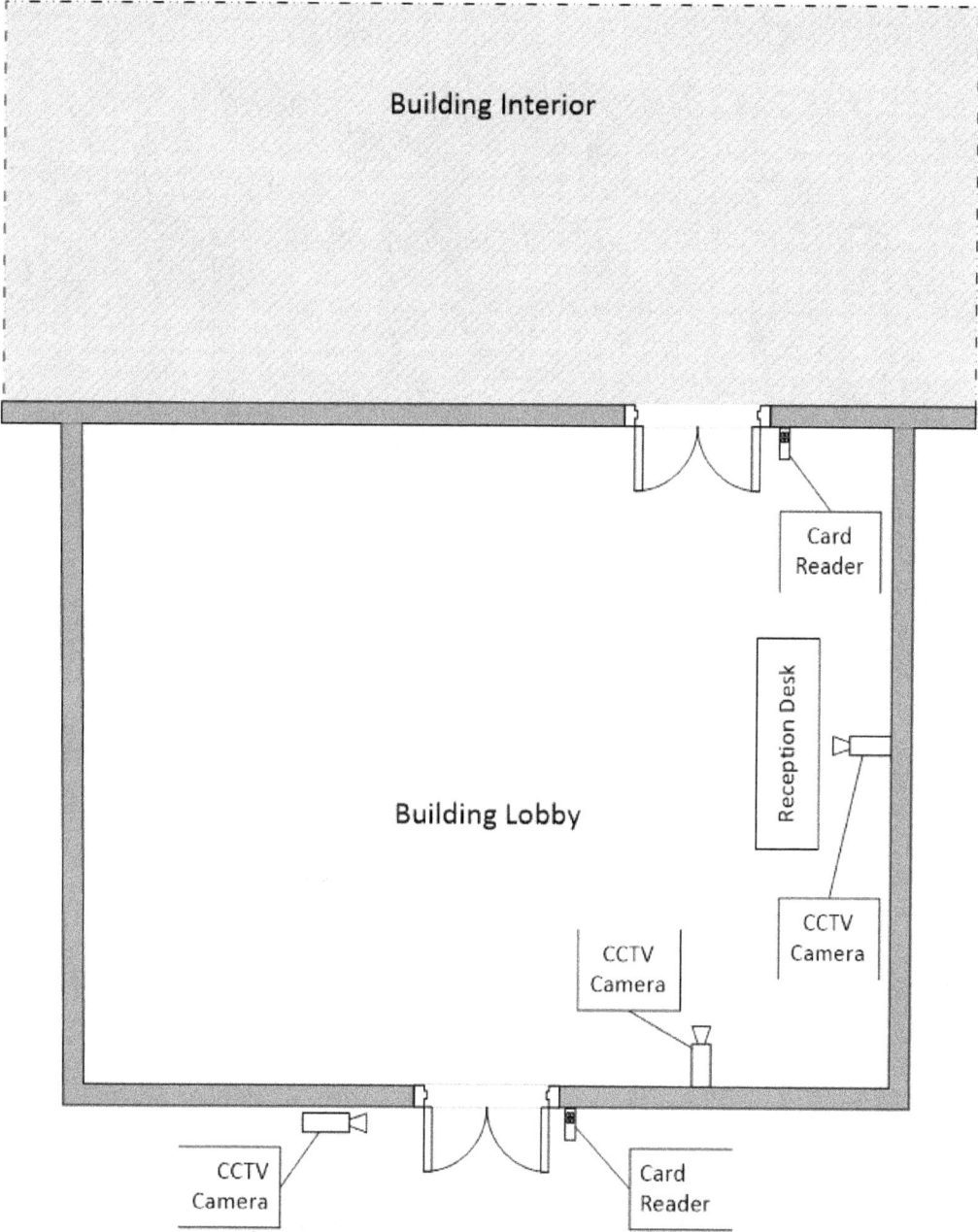

Figure 18: Sample Building Lobby Layout – B (Not to Scale)

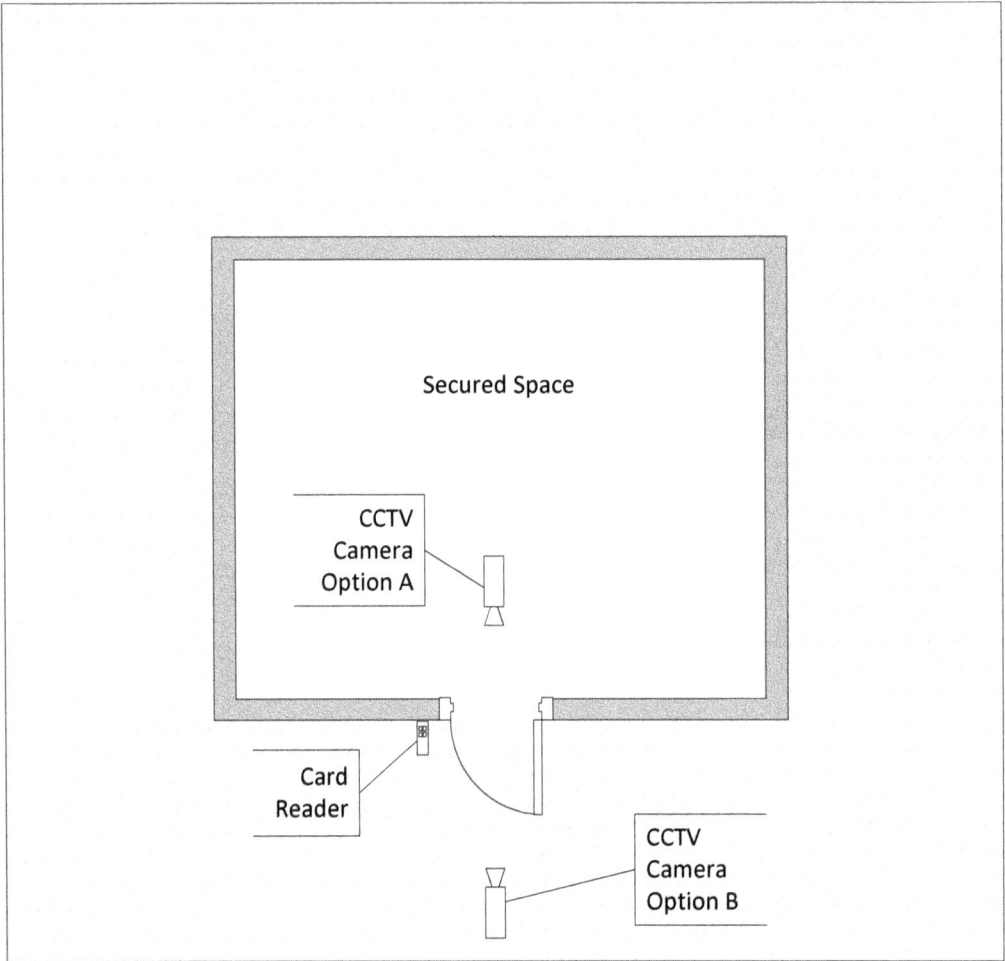

Figure 19: Sample Secured Space (Not to Scale)

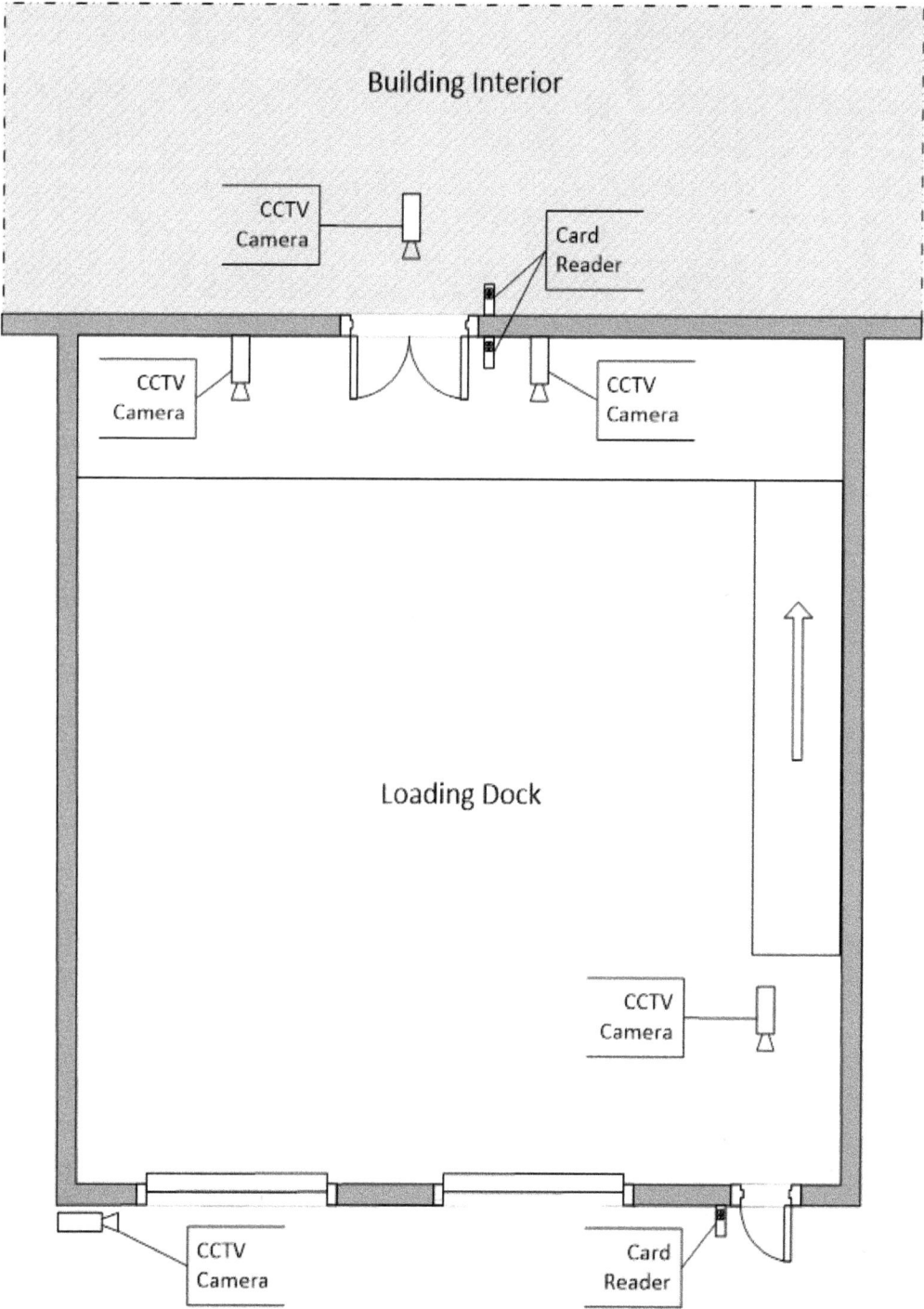

Figure 20: Sample Loading Dock Layout (Not to Scale)

Appendix B

Emergency Procedures Checklists

Emergency procedures checklists serve as a supplement to a company's emergency procedures guidelines and are used to gather important incident specific information that can assist security, emergency response teams and managers in initiating appropriate response at the onset of an incident. While the following checklists provide emergency response guidelines, such as call 911 or initiate emergency evacuation, they are not intended to serve as all-encompassing emergency procedures. Managers may choose to use these checklists to supplement their existing emergency procedures or as a basis upon which to develop more comprehensive site specific emergency procedures manuals.

FIRE ALARM

Date:	Time:
Caller's Name:	**Callback Number:**

Location: Bldg: Floor: Area\Room Name or #:

Alarm Type:

☐ Smoke Detector   ☐ Heat Detector   ☐ Pull Station   ☐ Sprinkler   ☐ Fire Pump

☐ Supervision\Trouble

Has fire department been notified?   ☐ Yes   ☐ No – Call 911

Is there a fire?   ☐ Yes – Call 911; Follow Fire Emergency Procedures   ☐ No

Has building been evacuated: ☐ Yes   ☐ No – Intitiate emergency evacuation procedures

Has all clear been give?   ☐ Yes – Allow reentry to building   ☐ No – Do not allow reentry

IMMEDIATE NOTIFICATIONS

Facilities Notification (Name)	Time Notified	Callback Time\Comments
Safety Notification (Name)	Time Notified	Callback Time\Comments
Security Notification (Name)	Time Notified	Callback Time\Comments

ESCALATION NOTIFICATIONS – ONLY AS DIRECTED

Fire Department	Time Notified	Time on Scene\Comments
Ambulance	Time Notified	Time on Scene\Comments
Other (Name)	Time Notified	Callback Time\Comments
Other (Name)	Time Notified	Callback Time\Comments

FIRE

Date: | **Time:**

Caller's Name: | **Callback Number:**

Location: Bldg: Floor: Area\Room Name or #:

Alarm Type:

☐ Smoke Detector   ☐ Heat Detector   ☐ Pull Station   ☐ Sprinkler   ☐ Fire Pump
☐ Supervision\Trouble

Has fire department been notified?   ☐ Yes   ☐ No – Call 911

Is there a fire?   ☐ Yes – Call 911; Follow Fire Emergency Procedures   ☐ No

Has building been evacuated: ☐ Yes   ☐ No – Intitiate emergency evacuation procedures

☐ **Fire**   ☐ **Smoke**   ☐ **Explosion**

Type Fire\Material Involved:

☐ Electrical   ☐ Equipment   ☐ Chemical   ☐ Fuel   ☐ Rubbish   ☐ Furniture   ☐ Vehicle

☐ Wood   ☐ Construction Materials   ☐ Brush\Forest   ☐ Other:

Extent of fire: ☐ Room\Area Only   ☐ Entire Floor   ☐ Entire Bldg.   ☐ Other:

Are occupants trapped in building?   ☐ No   ☐ Yes – # of people: ; Location:

Are there injuries: ☐ No   ☐ Yes – # of people: ; Location:

Is there personnel Hazmat exposure?   ☐ Yes – complete info below   ☐ No

Type Exposure: ☐ Inhalation   ☐ Contact – body part affected?

Material Type: ☐ Biological   ☐ Chemical   ☐ Radiological

Are people being decontaminated?   ☐ Eyewash Station   ☐ Emergency Shower   ☐ Other

Where:

IMMEDIATE NOTIFICATIONS

Facilities Notification (Name)	Time Notified	Callback Time\Comments
Safety Notification (Name)	Time Notified	Callback Time\Comments
Security Notification (Name)	Time Notified	Callback Time\Comments

ESCALATION NOTIFICATIONS – ONLY AS DIRECTED

Fire Department	Time Notified	Time on Scene\Comments
Other (Name)	Time Notified	Callback Time\Comments

MEDICAL EMERGENCY

Date:	Time:
Caller's Name:	Callback Number:

Location: Bldg: Floor: Area\Room Name or #:

Is the victim conscious? ☐ Yes   ☐ No – Call 911

What is the nature of the injury?

Is this a life threatening injury? ☐ Yes – Call 911   ☐ No

What body part is affected?
☐ Arm\Hand ☐ Leg\Foot ☐ Head\Neck ☐ Face\Eyes\Mouth ☐ Back ☐ Chest
☐ Abdomen

Is the person bleeding? ☐ No ☐ Yes – Is it being controlled? **Yes \ No**

Are there any broken bones or crush injuries? ☐ Yes ☐ No

Is victim trapped by equipment or materials? ☐ No ☐ Yes – Describe:

Has or is First Aid\CPR\AED being administered? ☐ No ☐ Yes – By Whom:

Is there personnel Hazmat exposure? ☐ Yes – complete info below ☐ No

Type Exposure: ☐ Inhalation   ☐ Contact – body part affected?

Material Type: ☐ Biological   ☐ Chemical   ☐ Radiological

Are people being decontaminated? ☐ Eyewash Station ☐ Emergency Shower ☐ Other

Where:

IMMEDIATE NOTIFICATIONS

Facilities Notification (Name)	Time Notified	Callback Time\Comments
Safety Notification (Name)	Time Notified	Callback Time\Comments
Security Notification (Name)	Time Notified	Callback Time\Comments

ESCALATION NOTIFICATIONS – ONLY AS DIRECTED

Fire Department	Time Notified	Time on Scene\Comments
Ambulance	Time Notified	Time on Scene\Comments
Other (Name)	Time Notified	Callback Time\Comments

HAZARDOUS MATERIAL SPILL\LEAK

Date:	Time:
Caller's Name:	Callback Number:

Location: Bldg: Floor: Area\Room Name or #:

Material Type: ☐ Biological ☐ Chemical ☐ Radiological
Material Name:

Material Charaacteristics: ☐ Liquid ☐ Solid ☐ Vapor ☐ Thick ☐ Runny **Color:**

NFPA Label Information: ◆ ◆ ◆ ◇

Other Hazard Label: ☐ Toxic ☐ Poison ☐ Corrosive ☐ Acid ☐ Other:

Approximate amount \ area covered?

Has spill been contained? ☐ Yes (spill kit?) ☐ No   **Is it spreading?** ☐ Yes ☐ No

What was the source of the spill \ leak?
☐ Equipment ☐ Container\Barrel ☐ Cabinet ☐ Vehicle ☐ Other:

Has area been barricaded? ☐ Yes (go to next)   ☐ No (restrict access to area)

Is there personnel Hazmat exposure? ☐ Yes – complete info below   ☐ No
Type Exposure: ☐ Inhalation ☐ Contact – body part affected?
Material Type: ☐ Biological ☐ Chemical ☐ Radiological
Are people being decontaminated? ☐ Eyewash Station ☐ Emergency Shower ☐ Other
Where:

IMMEDIATE NOTIFICATIONS

Facilities Notification (Name)	Time Notified	Callback Time\Comments
Safety Notification (Name)	Time Notified	Callback Time\Comments
Security Notification (Name)	Time Notified	Callback Time\Comments

ESCALATION NOTIFICATIONS – ONLY AS DIRECTED

Fire Department	Time Notified	Time on Scene\Comments
Ambulance	Time Notified	Time on Scene\Comments
Other (Name)	Time Notified	Callback Time\Comments

WATER LEAK

Date:	Time:
Caller's Name:	Callback Number:

Location: Bldg: Floor: Area\Room Name or #:

Type Leak:

☐ Equipment\Machinery – Type\Asset Tag #: _____

☐ Roof ☐ Pipe ☐ Window\Door ☐ Other:

Extent of Leak: ☐ Immediate Area ☐ Area Only ☐ Entire Floor ☐ Multiple Floors

Extent of Damage: ☐ Equipment ☐ Carpet\Floor ☐ Walls ☐ Furniture ☐ Boxes

Other Hazard Label: ☐ Toxic ☐ Poison ☐ Corrosive ☐ Acid ☐ Other:

Are hazardous materials affected? ☐ Yes – complete info below ☐ No

Material Type: ☐ Biological ☐ Chemical ☐ Radiological

Material Properties: ☐ Liquid ☐ Solid ☐ Gas

Material Name:

IMMEDIATE NOTIFICATIONS

	Time Notified	Callback Time\Comments
Facilities Notification (Name)		
Safety Notification (Name)		
Security Notification (Name)		

ESCALATION NOTIFICATIONS – ONLY AS DIRECTED

	Time Notified	Time on Scene\Comments
Water Company		
Fire Department		
Other (Name)		Callback Time\Comments
Other (Name)		Callback Time\Comments
Other (Name)		Callback Time\Comments

POWER FAILURE \ SURGE

Date:	Time:
Caller's Name:	Callback Number:

Location: Bldg: Floor: Area\Room Name or #:

Extent of Outage:

☐ Area\Room Only   ☐ Entire Floor   ☐ Multiple Floors   ☐ Single Building

☐ Multiple Buildings   ☐ Community Wide

Is emergency generator running: ☐ Yes   ☐ No

Are emergency lights on?   ☐ Yes   ☐ No

Are security systems operational?   ☐ Yes   ☐ No – Describe:

Are computer systems operational?   ☐ Yes   ☐ No

IMMEDIATE NOTIFICATIONS		
Facilities Notification (Name)	Time Notified	Callback Time\Comments
Safety Notification (Name)	Time Notified	Callback Time\Comments
Security Notification (Name)	Time Notified	Callback Time\Comments

ESCALATION NOTIFICATIONS – ONLY AS DIRECTED		
Utility Company (Name)	Time Notified	Time on Scene\Comments
Other (Name)	Time Notified	Calback Time\Comments
Other (Name)	Time Notified	Callback Time\Comments
Other (Name)	Time Notified	Callback Time\Comments
Other (Name)	Time Notified	Callback Time\Comments
Other (Name)	Time Notified	Callback Time\Comments

ELEVATOR ENTRAPMENT

Date:	Time:
Caller's Name:	Callback Number:

Location: Bldg: Floor:

Elevator Number:	Where is it stuck?

Number of persons in elevator:	Any injuries or medical conditions? ☐ Yes ☐ No

Are emergency lights on? ☐ Yes   ☐ No

Describe injuries or medical conditions:

IMMEDIATE NOTIFICATIONS

Facilities Notification (Name)	Time Notified	Callback Time\Comments
Safety Notification (Name)	Time Notified	Callback Time\Comments
Security Notification (Name)	Time Notified	Callback Time\Comments
Elevator Service Company (Name)	Time Notified	Time on Scene\Comments

ESCALATION NOTIFICATIONS – ONLY AS DIRECTED

Fire Department	Time Notified	Time on Scene\Comments
Ambulance	Time Notified	Time on Scene\Comments
Other (Name)	Time Notified	Callback Time\Comments
Other (Name)	Time Notified	Callback Time\Comments

BUILDING SYSTEMS ALARM \ FAILURE

Date:	Time:
Caller's Name:	Callback Number:

Location: Bldg: Floor: Area\Room Name or #:

Equipment Type:

☐ HVAC   ☐ Compressor   ☐ Gas Monitor\Oxygen Sensor   ☐ Generator   ☐ Electrical

☐ PH Level\Waste Water   ☐ Water Pump   ☐ Other:

Set Point:	Acceptable Variance:	Actual Reading:

Is it a hazardous material area? ☐ Yes   ☐ No

Are there any fluid leaks: ☐ No   ☐ Yes – Describe:

Are there any unusual odors: ☐ No   ☐ Yes – Describe:

Remarks:

IMMEDIATE NOTIFICATIONS

Facilities Notification (Name)	Time Notified	Callback Time\Comments
Safety Notification (Name)	Time Notified	Callback Time\Comments
Security Notification (Name)	Time Notified	Callback Time\Comments

ESCALATION NOTIFICATIONS – ONLY AS DIRECTED

Other (Name)	Time Notified	Calback Time\Comments
Other (Name)	Time Notified	Callback Time\Comments
Other (Name)	Time Notified	Callback Time\Comments
Other (Name)	Time Notified	Callback Time\Comments
Other (Name)	Time Notified	Callback Time\Comments

SEVERE WEATHER ALERT

Date:	Start Time:	End Time:

How was alert received? ☐ Radio ☐ Weather Website ☐ Other Media:

Condition: ☐ Advisory ☐ Warning ☐ Alert

Type:

☐ Tornado\Hurricane ☐ Lightening ☐ High Winds ☐ Heavy Rain ☐ Hail

☐ Flooding ☐ Winter Storm\Blizzard ☐ Other:

Affected Counties\Cities:

Has call to shelter been ordered? ☐ Yes ☐ No	Time Given:	Time All Clear:

Remarks:

IMMEDIATE NOTIFICATIONS

Facilities Notification (Name)	Time Notified	Callback Time\Comments
Safety Notification (Name)	Time Notified	Callback Time\Comments
Security Notification (Name)	Time Notified	Callback Time\Comments

ESCALATION NOTIFICATIONS – ONLY AS DIRECTED

Other (Name)	Time Notified	Calback Time\Comments
Other (Name)	Time Notified	Callback Time\Comments
Other (Name)	Time Notified	Callback Time\Comments
Other (Name)	Time Notified	Callback Time\Comments
Other (Name)	Time Notified	Callback Time\Comments

SUSPICIOUS ITEM \ PACKAGE

Date:	Time:
Caller's Name: (ask for spelling)	**Callback Number:**

Location: Bldg: Floor: Area\Room Name or #:

Item Type:

☐ Parcel\Package   ☐ Letter   ☐ Box   ☐ Backpack   ☐ Bag   ☐ Box   ☐ Laptop Bag

☐ Handbag   ☐ Tool Box   ☐ Lunch Box   ☐ Other:

Distinguishing Characteristics:

☐ Exposed Wiring   ☐ Leaking   ☐ Bulging   ☐ Excessive Postage   ☐ Excessive Taping

☐ Strong Odor   ☐ Improperly Addressed   ☐ No Return Address   ☐ Other:

Item Description\Comments:

Has access to area been restricted: ☐ Yes   ☐ **No** – Restrict access to area

IMMEDIATE NOTIFICATIONS

Facilities Notification (Name)	Time Notified	Callback Time\Comments
Safety Notification (Name)	Time Notified	Callback Time\Comments
Security Notification (Name)	Time Notified	Callback Time\Comments

ESCALATION NOTIFICATIONS – ONLY AS DIRECTED

Police Department	Time Notified	Time on Scene\Comments
Fire Department	Time Notified	Time on Scene\Comments
Other (Name)	Time Notified	Callback Time\Comments
Other (Name)	Time Notified	Callback Time\Comments

BOMB THREAT CHECKLIST (Page 1)

Date:	Time:
Caller's Name\Received By:	Callback Number or Caller ID on Phone:

Caller's Exact Words Type:

Ask Questions:

a) When is the bomb going to explode?

b) Where is the bomb right now (Building, Floor, Area)?

c) What kind of bomb is it?

d) What does it look like?

e) Why did you place the bomb?

f) How is the bomb going to be detonated?

g) What is your name?

Caller Identity: Male ☐   Female ☐   Adult ☐   Juvenile ☐   Approx. Age:

Voice Characteristics:

Loud ☐   Soft ☐   High Pitched ☐   Deep ☐   Raspy ☐   Pleasant ☐   Intoxicated ☐

Other:

Accent: Local ☐   Foreign ☐   Region:

Speech:

Fast ☐   Slow ☐   Distinct ☐   Distorted ☐   Stutter ☐   Nasal ☐

Slurred ☐   Lisp ☐

Language:

Excellent ☐   Good ☐   Fair ☐   Poor ☐   Foul ☐   Other:

Manner:

Calm ☐   Angry ☐   Rational ☐   Irrational ☐   Coherent ☐   Incoherent ☐

Deliberate ☐   Emotional ☐   Righteous ☐   Laughing ☐

Background Noises:

Office Sounds ☐   Factory Sounds ☐   Trains ☐   Airplanes ☐   Street Traffic ☐

Music ☐   Voices ☐   Party Atmosphere ☐   Bedlam ☐   Animals ☐   Mixed ☐

Quiet ☐

BOMB THREAT CHECKLIST (Page 2)

IMMEDIATE NOTIFICATIONS

Facilities Notification (Name)	Time Notified	Callback Time\Comments
Safety Notification (Name)	Time Notified	Callback Time\Comments
Security Notification (Name)	Time Notified	Callback Time\Comments

ESCALATION NOTIFICATIONS – ONLY AS DIRECTED

Police Department	Time Notified	Time on Scene\Comments
Fire Department	Time Notified	Time on Scene\Comments
Other (Name)	Time Notified	Callback Time\Comments
Other (Name)	Time Notified	Callback Time\Comments
Other (Name)	Time Notified	Callback Time\Comments
Other (Name)	Time Notified	Callback Time\Comments

Additional Comments:

ACTIVE SHOOTER

Date:	Time:
Caller's Name:	Callback Number:

Location: Bldg: Floor: Area\Room Name or #:

NOTIFY POLICE \ 911

How many shooters are there?

What type of weapons does the shooter(s) have?
☐ Handgun   ☐ Rifle   ☐ Shotgun   ☐ Explosive Device   ☐ Other:

SHOOTER DESCRIPTION

Does anyone know the shooter? ☐ No   ☐ Yes – Name:

Sex: ☐ Male ☐ Female ☐ Unknown	**Race:** ☐ White ☐ Black ☐ Hispanic ☐ Asian ☐ Other:
Age: ☐ Under 18 ☐ 18 – 25 ☐ 26 – 35 ☐ 35 – 50 ☐ Over 50 ☐ Unknown	**Body Build:** ☐ Slender ☐ Medium ☐ Muscular ☐ Overweight ☐ Obese ☐ Unknown

Clothing Description (include color and any logos):
☐ Hat:_____   ☐ Collared Shirt: _____   ☐ Sweat Shirt:_____
☐ T-Shirt:_____   ☐ Pants:_____   ☐ Hat:_____   ☐ Shoes:_____

VICTIM INFORMATION

How many people are injured?

Is First Aid\CPR\AED being administered? ☐ Yes   ☐ No

IMMEDIATE NOTIFICATIONS

Police	Time Notified	Time on Time\Comments
Security (Name)	Time Notified	Callback Time\Comments
Facility Mangement (Name)	Time Notified	Callback Time\Comments

ESCALATION NOTIFICATIONS – ONLY AS DIRECTED

Other	Time Notified	Time on Scene\Comments
Other	Time Notified	Time on Scene\Comments

Appendix C

References and Resource Links

References

1   Crime Prevention Through Environmental Design (CPTED)
     http://www.cptedsecurity.com/cpted_design_guidelines.htm

2   National Fire Protection Association Life Safety Code (NFPA-101)
     https://www.nfpa.org/codes-and-standards/all-codes-and-standards/list-
     of-codes-and-standards/detail?code=101

3   International Building Code, Chapter 10, Means of Egress
     https://www2.iccsafe.org/states/oregon/building/2004_PDFs/Chapter_10
     _Means%20of%20Egress.pdf

4   29 CFR 1910, U.S. Occupational Health & Safety Administration (OSHA),
     Uniform Building Code
     https://www.osha.gov/SLTC/firesafety/standards.html

5   29 CFR 1910.38, U.S. Occupational Health & Safety Administration (OSHA),
     Emergency Action Plans
     https://www.osha.gov/pls/oshaweb/owadisp.show_document?p_table=S
     TANDARDS&p_id=9726

6   21 CFR – Food and Drugs
     https://www.fda.gov/MedicalDevices/DeviceRegulationandGuidance/Dat
     abases/ucm135680.htm

7   Customs Trade Partnership Against Terrorism (CTPAT)
     https://www.cbp.gov/border-security/ports-entry/cargo-security/ctpat

8   SSAE No. 18, Statement on Standards for Attestation Engagements
        https://www.aicpa.org/Research/Standards/AuditAttest/DownloadableD
        ocuments/SSAE_No_18.pdf

9   International Organization for Standardization (ISO) 27001 and 27002
        http://www.27000.org/

10   Transportation Asset Protection Association (TAPA)
        http://www.tapaonline.org/

11   The Battle: Human vs Machine, Hi-Tech Security Solutions Magazine, CCTV,
        Surveillance & Remote Monitoring, Oct 2017
        http://www.securitysa.com/8158r

12   Simon, H. A. (1971) "Designing Organizations for an Information-Rich
        World" in: Martin Greenberger, Computers, *Communication, and the Public
        Interest, Baltimore*. MD: The Johns Hopkins Press. pp. 40–41

13   U.S. Federal Emergency Management Agency (FEMA) Business Webpage
        https://www.ready.gov/business

14   FEMA online media library
        https://www.fema.gov/media-library#{}

15   U.S. Department of Homeland Security Exercise and Evaluation Program
        (HSEEP) https://www.fema.gov/media-library/assets/documents/32326)

16   National Fire Protection Association (NFPA®) 1600, Standard on
        Disaster/Emergency Management and Business Continuity Programs:
        http://www.nfpa.org/codes-and-standards)

17   Corporate Emergency Access System
        http://www.ceas.com/

18   The Psychology And Philosophy Of Branding, Marketing, Needs, And
        Actions, Forbes, Mar 2014
        https://www.forbes.com/sites/work-in-progress/2014/03/05/the-
        psychology-and-philosophy-of-branding-marketing-needs-and-
        actions/#433c3f79725a

19   U.S. Federal Bureau of Investigation, How to spot a possible insider threat.
        https://www.fbi.gov/news/stories/how-to-spot-a-possible-insider-threat

20   DuPont & Widener IP CLE, Trade Secret Proceedings at the International
      Trade Commission
      https://www.crowell.com/files/Trade-Secret-Proceedings-at-the-ITC-
      Recent-Developments-Post-TianRui.pdf

21   Society for Competitive Intelligence
      http://www.scip.org/

22   Semantic™ blog, Social Engineering Fundamentals, Part I: Hacker Tactics
      http://www.securityfocus.com/infocus/1527

23   The Company Man: Protecting America's Secrets:
      https://www.fbi.gov/news/stories/economic-espionage

Additional Resource Links

Facility Security

U.S. Department of Homeland Security National Infrastructure Protection Plan
https://www.dhs.gov/national-infrastructure-protection-plan

U.S. Defense Security Service Self-Inspection Handbook for NISP Contractors,
http://www.cdse.edu/documents/cdse/self_inspect_handbook_nisp.pdf

U.S. Department of Defense (DoD) Manual 5220.22-M, National Industrial
Security Program Operating Manual (NISPOM)
http://www.dss.mil/documents/odaa/nispom2006-5220.pdf

American Society for Industrial Security (ASIS)
https://www.asisonline.org/Pages/default.aspx

Supply Chain Security

U.S. Federal Bureau of Investigations Cargo Theft User Manual
https://ucr.fbi.gov/cargo-theft-user-manual

Emergency Response and Preparedness

National Fire Protection Association (NFPA®) 1600, Standard on Disaster/Emergency Management and Business Continuity Programs
https://www.nfpa.org/assets/files/AboutTheCodes/1600/1600-13-PDF.pdf

Travel Security

U.S. Department of State – Bureau of Consular Affairs
https://travel.state.gov/content/travel.html

U.S. Centers for Disease Control and Prevention – Traveler's Health
https://wwwnc.cdc.gov/travel

Personal Security & Emergency Preparedness

Personal\home emergency preparedness planning
https://www.ready.gov/

Child Safety

- US Federal Trade Commission - Protecting Kids Online
  https://www.consumer.ftc.gov/topics/protecting-kids-online

- FBI Parent Resources: https://www.fbi.gov/resources/parents

- Be Internet Awesome
  https://beinternetawesome.withgoogle.com/?utm_source=keyword&utm_medium=blog-pr&utm_campaign=bia-blog

- Netsmartz Kids: http://www.netsmartzkids.org/

- McGruff Just for Kids: https://www.mcgruffstuff.com/

Identify Theft & Fraud

- U.S. Federal Trade Commission, Consumer Information
  https://www.consumer.ftc.gov/

- U.S. Federal Bureau of Investigations, Common Fraud Schemes
  (internet, business, credit card, fraud against seniors, etc.)
  https://www.fbi.gov/scams-and-safety/common-fraud-schemes

www.ingramcontent.com/pod-product-compliance
Lightning Source LLC
Chambersburg PA
CBHW080622030426
42336CB00018B/3046